SURVIVING AND THRIVING

365 facts

IN BLACK ECONOMIC HISTORY

SURVIVING AND THRIVING

365 *facts* IN BLACK ECONOMIC HISTORY

Julianne Malveaux

[signature]

FOREWORD BY CATHY HUGHES

Last Word Productions, Inc.
Washington, D.C.

Last Word Productions, Inc.
1220 L Street NW, STE 100 #197
Washington, DC 20005

First Edition   Paperback
Printed in the United States of America

Book layout and design by Borel Graphics
Front photography for collage by istock.com, Madam Walker, March on Washington and A. Philip Randolph courtesy of Library of Congress Prints and Photographs Division, Washington, DC

ISBN 978-0-9827750-0-4
12 11 10   5 4 3 2 1

African-American Studies | United States History | Economics | Labor
Non-fiction
Foreword by Cathy Hughes

www.lastwordprod.com

DEDICATION

This book is dedicated to the memory of my family surviving, thriving, and enjoying life,
Especially to my great aunt, Annie Mae Randall,
Who taught and thrived in segregated Moss Point, Mississippi,
Who endured the loss of land when our family's land was expropriated for public space –
Now it's "Hawkins Lane" –
And to her siblings: Grandmother Rose Elizabeth Nelson, Great Aunt Mary Louise Hammond, Great Uncle Sam Hawkins, and Great Uncle Clarence Hawkins. These are the shoulders on which I stand.

ACKNOWLEDGMENTS

I taught a Black Economic History Class at the University of California, Berkeley's African-American Studies Department in the early 1990s. My students were irreverent and challenging. Once a student told me that I had not offered enough examples of slave resistance to oppression, and this comment sent me into library stacks to expand on the most frequent examples of Nat Turner and Denmark Vesey. Another student asked about the contradictions of "self-purchase" with a catch in her throat which so affected me it has influenced my work to this day. Among the many I must thank for their inspiration, support, and friendship in the production of this book, I am grateful to the many students who have asked the pointed questions that have stimulated this work.

I am also grateful to colleagues in the economics profession who continue to do the work needed for closing racial economic gaps, especially William "Sandy" Darity, Ron Johnson, Margaret Simms, Bernard Anderson, and Rhonda Sharpe.

Teamwork makes the dream work. This project has been a dream of mine for nearly 20 years, but it would not have been completed but for the dedicated and committed work of a thoughtful and aggressive team. Patrick Oliver took my initial concept and expanded it. He also managed this project with patience and grace. I am so very grateful to Patrick for his work. To describe Miracle Howard simply as project coordinator and researcher does not do her efforts justice. She tracked down facts and photos indefatigably, managed schedules seamlessly, worked evenings and weekends, and showed an amazing commitment to this project. I am most grateful to her. Charnice Milton was a tireless researcher and a delightful

ACKNOWLEDGMENTS_____

soul. The gruff Donald Harrington provided transportation services for the team, shared Washington, DC oral history, and injected humor into long days of work.

Our production team was amazing, and a key part of it was the work that Denise Borel Billups, at Borel Graphics, did. She "got" the concept, design and energy and she translated it graphically, from the colors to the cover. She worked tirelessly with our team to ensure that every period, comma, and semicolon was correct. She worked nights and she worked weekends and she brought a precious energy and enthusiasm to our work. Thank you, Denise.

My thanks are no less heartfelt for the editorial team of Elliot Bratton, Randall Horton, Leola Dublin, Antoinette Brim, and De'Lana Dameron. I appreciate their skills in the production of this project.

We are indebted to the many librarians who were generous with their time in helping us locate photos, especially colleagues at the Martin Luther King, Jr. Library in Washington, DC, the Library of Congress, and Mary Yearwood, Antony Touissant and Tom Lisanti at the Schomburg Center for Research in Black Culture.

Several individuals also offered photographs, and I am grateful to all of them, especially Andrea Harris, of the North Carolina Minority Business Development Institute. Also, ALélia Bundles, great-great-granddaughter and biographer of Madame C.J. Walker.

I am also grateful to those who offered book endorsements, including Dr. Juliet E.K. Walker, Dr. Avis Jones-Deweever, Jeff Johnson, and Hazel Trice Edney. Special thanks to Cathy Hughes who has been an inspiration as a communicator and entrepreneur. With everything she has on her plate, I appreciate the time she took to write the foreword to this book.

If I have overlooked anyone in offering thanks and acknowledgments, I would ask them to charge it to my head and not to my heart. The development and completion of this project reminds me of how intertwined we all are, a lesson that our foremothers and fathers learned when they were chained together in the holds of slave ships. Thus, I want to take no favor for granted and to acknowledge every kindness.

Finally, I want to thank my family and friends for supporting me in this work, and in all of the work that I do. I am especially grateful to my sister, Mariette Malveaux, whose unconditional love and support is a blessing and source of my strength.

Contents

CONTENTS

• Week 8 •

• Week 9 •

• Week 10 •

• Week 11 •

Contents

CONTENTS_____

CONTENTS

365 *facts* IN BLACK ECONOMIC HISTORY |

CONTENTS_____

Contents

CONTENTS_____

_____Contents

• Week 40 •

• Week 41 •

• Week 42 •

• Week 43 •

CONTENTS_____

CONTENTS_____

FOREWORD BY CATHY HUGHES

Surviving and Thriving

© Cathy Hughes.

Black folk have never played on a level field where the economy is concerned. We have been propertied more frequently than we have held property. We have been exploited more frequently than we have been empowered. We have been 'buked and we have been scorned. Nonetheless, to quote Dr. Maya Angelou, "and still we rise."

In other words, we have been a viable collective to dictate economic stimulus and create communal wealth. We have started businesses and, through our boycotts, we have stopped them. We are a people who have gone far by faith, playing the game even when the rules weren't fair. From the moments when enslaved Blacks decided to buy their own freedom to the moments when some of us chose to trade our businesses on Wall Street, we have been bold, bodacious, and brilliant. We have both survived and thrived. I am so very pleased with this little jewel that Julianne Malveaux has put together. As an economist, she has always been passionate about the economic activity of our people. Now she has found 365 economic history facts – one a day – that can be used to motivate and inspire. She is speaking to future generations who need to know that there are shoulders to stand on as we continue to grow economically. To be sure, there are racial economic gaps which need to be closed. At the same time, there are stories of tenacity that must compel us to continue to strive to create wealth.

As the founder of Radio One and TV One, I can sincerely appreciate *Surviving and Thriving: 365 facts in Black Economic History.* The recording and documenting of our economic development is critical to our continued growth. What makes this book special is that every member of the household can read it. Julianne Malveaux gets straight to the point with her facts. Parents, when you send your kids to school in the morning, give them a fact for the day to instill a sense of history, a sense of pride. I am excited to have this book in my possession and will give it as a gift on birthdays, on Christmas, and on any opportunity I get for enlightenment. I view it as an investment in the economic development of the folks I care about.

Our story has been one of triumph and tragedy in America. This is a book which highlights the personal achievements and tragedies associated with Black economic development. It spotlights our losses that were the result of racial economic envy, as when Tulsa, Oklahoma was bombed via air attack to destroy a thriving community in 1921. But there have been many sweet moments, such as Reggie Lewis's leadership of Beatrice Foods and the powerful empire amassed by Madame C.J. Walker.

| XXIII |

And so we rise, and so we thrive. I am grateful to Dr. Julianne Malveaux for this needed work and am thankful to have played some small part in our nation's Black economic history.

Cathy Liggins Hughes
Founder, Radio One/TV One

Introduction by Julianne Malveaux

From Free Frank To Billionaires and Beyond

The History of African American Economic Empowerment

When people think of African-Americans and the economy, the image that may come to mind is that of a child with her nose pressed against the window of a candy store – of someone who has been placed at the periphery, locked away from the goodies that come with economic participation. Aggregate data unfortunately bear this image out: the African-American unemployment rate is nearly twice that of Whites, 16.3 percent, compared to 8.7 percent for Whites in August of this year. Poverty among African-Americans is almost three times worse than for Whites – 24.7 percent compared to 8.6 percent in 2008. Household income is only 60 percent as high – $34,218 for African-Americans and $55,530 for Whites; and while African-American people are 13 percent of the total population, we hold less than three percent of the nation's wealth. [1]

The Great Recession that began in 2008 has reinforced the aggregate peripheral status of African-Americans in the economy. According to the Center for Responsible Lending, African-Americans and Latinos, who already lag in terms of income, wealth, and educational attainment, are disproportionately vulnerable to the foreclosure crisis. While 14.8 percent of non-Hispanic Whites were in danger of foreclosure in June 2010, the risk for African-Americans and Latinos exceeded 21 percent. The Center for Responsible Lending estimates that between $177 and $194 billion will be drained from black and brown communities between 2009 and 2012 as a result of foreclosures and their spillover losses. [2]

And yet, African-Americans have survived in depression, recession, and recovery. Despite daunting negative statistics, the story of Black Economic History is a story of both surviving and thriving, of a people who have been determined to participate in a game that was skewed against them. The playing field has never been level for African-Americans, yet even with the slant, we have been players and often winners. We have also been integral parts of the economic history of our nation, contributing to economic growth and development in ways that are rarely acknowledged.

Economics is the study of who gets what, when, where, and why. It is the study of the way that the factors of production – land, labor, capital, and creativity – are paid in rent, wages, interest, and profit. It is the history of the knife, of how the pie is sliced. And it is the story of why African-Americans get so much less than our share of that pie, and so much less credit for our economic participation in this nation.

The basic tenet that factors of production are given factor payments worked against African-Americans since 1619, when the first Africans held in bondage landed on these shores. While White itinerant workers were paid wages on a current or delayed basis (when they were indentured servants and had to pay back the price of their passage to the New World), Black workers, being enslaved, became a source of wealth for others. This point hits home when one visits the Underground Railroad Museum in Cincinnati, Ohio and views the exhibits outside the historic slave pen that was owned by Kentucky slave trader Col. John W. Anderson. Anderson held enslaved people in the pen, and the chains he used to secure them are part of the exhibit. On display is a page of his will, with the inventory of the people he enslaved and their value exhibited. There are names, descriptions, and prices for Black people. While some people in our nation were amassing wealth, other people were the wealth they amassed. How could the playing field ever level off in our nation when its very foundation is poisoned by the abomination of a system that dehumanized millions and relegated them to the status of property?

However, the Underground Railroad Museum also records the economic triumphs that some Black people experienced, even during the era of enslavement. Consider, for example, the case of John Parker, a Black abolitionist who lived in Ripley, Ohio along the Ohio River. According to his diaries, Parker was responsible for helping to free at least nine hundred slaves, helping them cross the Ohio River and connecting them with the Underground Railroad so they would be bound for Canada. Parker's story is all the more poignant because he was born into slavery, with an enslaved mother and a White father. Born in Norwalk, Virginia in 1827, he was just eight years old when he was sold, chained to an older man who was beaten to death, then brought further South as part of a chain gang.

At the young age of 14, Parker entered into a contract to buy his freedom for $1800. Free at 18, he moved from Mobile, Alabama to New Albany, Indiana. He owned a profitable iron foundry business, and patented a clod-smashing machine. He worked tirelessly to build his businesses by day, and by night he worked tirelessly to help free slaves, using force if necessary. Slave owners put a price on his head, and because of the Fugitive Slave Act, which allowed slave owners to cross into "free" territory to reclaim their "property," he might have lost all of his property if he were convicted of violating the law. Worse than that, Parker might have been re-enslaved (many free Blacks were abducted and sold into slavery, even though they had manumission papers), or even killed. He took the risk willingly and courageously, and empowered hundreds as they fled for their freedom. After the Civil War, John Parker became wealthy upon obtaining patents for agricultural equipment and expanding his foundry. [3]

This successful businessman and courageous abolitionist had to purchase himself. Whenever I write or speak these words, something twists in my stomach, and I am stunned by the awful contradiction of being forced to buy yourself. To purchase yourself! It is your self. Your own self. And yet it is a self you have to purchase if you want your freedom. What faith must one have had in order to enter into a contract with a slave owner, especially after the Supreme Court ruled against Dred Scott in 1857? The Court said that Black people had no rights which Whites were bound to respect, had no ability to enter into contracts, and no need to be governed by laws that divided our nation into slave and free. Buying yourself is like cutting a deal with the devil, because massa could always change the rules of the game, and then what recourse would the enslaved person (with no rights Whites are bound to respect) have? And yet, thousands of enslaved people of African descent purchased themselves. We know some of their names, and we know that history swallowed the names and lives of others, because history belongs to those who hold the pen. Formerly enslaved people were too busy surviving to write the story of their triumphs, and that is part of the reason that I was so passionate about compiling this book, *Surviving and Thriving: 365 Facts in Black Economic History.*

Because history belongs to those with the pen, these facts are not exhaustive. We know about John Parker and Free Frank McWorter, but there is less information about the laundry women who washed clothes for working class Whites week after week, saving their pennies until they were able to buy their freedom. Gender often shapes the stories we tell, and the gender bias of the 18th and 19th centuries means that more men's stories have survived than women's have. The story of Elizabeth Keckley, a St. Louis seamstress, is one of the women's stories that has survived. Her needle was the near-sole support of the White family that owned her; with help from some of her wealthy clients, she was able to raise the $1200 needed for her freedom. She was later seamstress to First Lady Mary Todd Lincoln and other prominent Washington, DC women.

We are indebted to Dr. Juliet E.K. Walker, an economic historian and a great-great-granddaughter of Free Frank McWorter, for painstakingly documenting his life, his challenges, and his triumphs. Free Frank was born in 1777 in South Carolina to an enslaved woman, Juda, and a planter, George McWhorter. When McWhorter moved to Kentucky, he took Frank to help him manage and build his landholdings. He also leased his son, Frank, to his neighbors. [4]

As a leased worker, Frank was able to save money and also develop his business skills. He used his savings to create a saltpeter mining and production operation, and with the money he earned from that manufacture, especially during the War of 1812, he purchased his freedom as well as that of his wife, Lucy, and 16 other family members. Along the way, he dropped the "H" from his last name, distinguishing himself from his master and former owner, George McWhorter.

Frank McWorter founded the town of New Philadelphia, Illinois in 1836. That interracial town was the first plotted and registered by an African-American. It is likely he moved to Illinois from Kentucky because of the oppressive conditions people of African descent experienced in Kentucky.

When he moved to Illinois, he left several family members behind and returned to Kentucky over the years to purchase them. Every time he returned, he put his life in danger, as slave trackers had no scruples about capturing and selling free African-Americans. Because he carried money, Free Frank was an attractive target for unscrupulous slave traders who would gain both his body and his cash. Still, he returned time and again, spending a total of $15,000 to free his relatives.

Free Frank died in 1854. His descendants used the money he left them to free seven more relatives. New Philadelphia was abandoned by 1885, and the town site is now farmland. It was placed on the National Register of Historic Places in 2005. Free Frank's grave had been included in the National Register in 1988. A great-great-granddaughter, Shirley McWorter-Moss, presented a life-size bronze bust of Free Frank to the Abraham Lincoln Presidential Library in 2008. Plans are underway to restore New Philadelphia.

The Free Frank story is especially inspirational because of McWorter's fealty to family, for his tenacity in both purchasing his relatives and creating wealth. It is a tribute to the entrepreneurial spirit embraced by some enslaved people who were determined to negotiate their freedom and that of their families in an oppressive capitalist system. Their lives are testaments to the fact that some people of African descent were able to win the game even when the rules weren't fair.

John Parker, Elizabeth Keckley, and Free Frank were exceptional but not unique. Indeed, tens of thousands of other enslaved people bought their freedom from their masters. In 1839, about 42 percent of the free Black people in Cincinnati, Ohio had bought their own freedom. [5] Countless others ran away, either to Canada or to northern states. Some were multi-generationally free, with their parents or grandparents having been freed by a sympathetic master or his will. In 1860, nearly 20 percent of the Black population of Washington, DC was free. [6]

Whether free or enslaved, African-American people were involved in the economic development of our nation. The nation's very own Capitol was built by enslaved people who were never paid for their work. Both the rice and cotton industries, the backbone of southern economic activity, were based on cultivation techniques developed on the African continent and introduced and improved by enslaved people here. And free and enslaved Black people were often passionate participants in entrepreneurship during slavery and in its aftermath.

Some of the early Black entrepreneurs were fur trappers. George Bonga, who lived in Duldo, Minnesota, was an interpreter in the signing of the Chippewa Treaty of 1837 and an independent entrepreneur who traded and trapped furs. Jean Baptiste Pointe du Sable, of Afro-Haitian ancestry, is often described as the founder of Chicago. Du Sable owned trading posts and was a fur trapper. James Forten was a sail-maker who patented a method for handling sails and grossed over $10,000 in 1832. Similarly, Paul Cuffe, a mathematician and navigator, earned more than $20,000 in fishing and trading in the same year. It is important to note that these independent entrepreneurs were often perceived as threatening by their White counterparts. When African-American men were involved in the trades, they were often not allowed to join trade unions. Still, there is significant evidence of economic involvement that transcended the simple quest for survival.

Some Black men and women were able to play prominent roles in economic leadership in the West. Notably, William Alexander Leidesdorff was the first African- American Treasurer of San Francisco (1847), and perhaps the nation's first Black millionaire. Born in St. Croix, Virgin Islands, he came to San Francisco just as it was being populated, operated the first steamboat, and was one of a committee of three who organized the city's first public school. A few years later, in 1852, Mary Ellen Pleasant, also known as "Mammy" Pleasant, arrived in San Francisco and became known as the "Mother of Civil Rights" in that city mostly because of a lawsuit, Pleasant v. North Beach that presaged Ida B. Wells' lawsuit against a railroad company in Tennessee. A wealthy woman, Pleasant was known for helping runaway slaves find employment and for championing civil rights causes. Because of her wealth, many Blacks and Whites were in her debt.

While African-Americans participated in the nation's economy prior to the end of slavery, they also were sidelined from many opportunities before the Civil War ended. Most notably, the Homestead Act of 1862 made up to 160 acres of settlement land available to citizens and even to those who intended to become citizens. The law blatantly favored new immigrants from Europe. This was a great opportunity for wealth building, an opportunity that enslaved people and other African-Americans were initially excluded from, however. At the same time, some African-Americans did establish all-Black towns, like Free Frank's New Philadelphia, or

Nicodemus, Kansas. Needless to say, those tenacious African-Americans who tried to carve out a space for themselves and their families were often met with hostility.

The achievements of individuals are often more prominently recorded by historians in the context of Black Economic History than the works of communities. Yet even during slavery, people of African descent formed churches and mutual aid societies and engaged in communal economic activity. These efforts were precursors of the Kwanzaa principle of Ujamaa (cooperative economics). For example, the Free African Union Society was founded in Newport, Rhode Island in the 1780s. The Free African Society was formed in Philadelphia in 1787. The African Benevolent Society was formed in Chillicothe, Ohio in 1827, and the New York African Society for Mutual Relief was formed in 1808. As a foundation of these societies, members contributed a weekly sum that was distributed to those in the group who were in need. Some societies also provided health and life insurance for their members. W.E.B. Du Bois described these societies as "the first wavering step of a people toward organized social life." Their formation is as much a part of Black Economic History as are the efforts so many made toward self-purchase – as oxymoronic as that phrase may be.

Thus, during the period of U.S. history in which enslavement was legal, African-Americans were economic participants and leaders. As abolitionists whose anti-slavery activities undermined the economic foundation of the South, and as community activists who strengthened the economic presence of Black people in the North, these were people and organizations of amazing distinction and phenomenal faith. After all, it must take a mighty faith to engage in trade (and especially trade involving one's very own person) with those who have defined one as less than human legally and morally. The faith and tenacity that African-Americans exhibited during this period must serve as an inspiration today when, despite a playing field that remains tilted, there are possibilities and opportunities for surviving and thriving.

Surviving and Thriving from Jim Crow to Civil Rights (1865-1964)

Slavery ended legal peonage, but it did not eliminate de facto peonage. Indeed, the legal end of slavery, absent the "forty acres and a mule" that was promised to give African-Americans an economic foothold, meant the start of a sharecropping system that effectively continued a method of enslavement. The end of slavery also did not mean the end of racism. Black Codes and Jim Crow laws restricted the movement of African- Americans as effectively as slavery once did. Some laws prevented African-Americans from owning land, the tools of their trade, and firearms. In some states, laws were passed to restrict the amount of cash that African-Americans could hold. At a time when the Homestead Act made land available to immigrants, some laws prevented African-Americans from purchasing land.

However, upon emancipation, formerly enslaved people began to organize banks and churches, colleges and insurance companies, newspapers and hospitals, and other organizations. The thirst for education and economic transformation was palpable, and dozens of historically Black colleges and universities (HBCUs) were organized before the turn of the century, funded in part by church contributions and bake sales, and buoyed by simple tenacity. My own beloved Bennett College for Women was organized in the unpaved basement of Warnersville (now St. Matthews) United Methodist Church by formerly enslaved people determined to be educated. Its original land was purchased with a $10,000 contribution by New York philanthropist Lyman Bennett. Reorganized by the United Methodist Women's Division as an all-women's college, this school has educated thousands of African-American women, played a pivotal role in the Civil Rights Movement, and been a significant economic force in Greensboro, North Carolina, most recently injecting more than $20 million into the local economy with a capital improvements program that has produced several new campus buildings.

Other HBCUs have had an important role in Black economic history. Tuskegee University, led by Booker T. Washington from 1881 until 1915, was a bastion of industrial education and economic self sufficiency. Tuskegee is the amazing institution that nurtured the inventor George Washington Carver in his research on the peanut, provided the training ground for the Tuskegee Airmen, and remains an important contemporary contributor to science and technology education and development.

The Freedmen's Bureau (formally known as the Bureau of Refugees, Freedmen and Abandoned Lands), authorized by the 1865 Freedmen's Bureau Bill, was charged with aiding formerly enslaved people with food and housing, education and health care, and employment contracts. It provided emergency aid to former slaves, helped to reunite families, and negotiated employment contracts between former slaves and former slaveholders. Most of the adminis- trators of the Freedmen's Bureau were northerners, described as "carpetbaggers" by former

Confederates. The first administrator of the Freedmen's Bureau was Union Army General Oliver O. Howard, the same man for whom Howard University is named. The Bureau operated from 1865 to 1872, with authority that diminished over the years. It was disbanded under President Ulysses Grant. While the Freedmen's Bureau was charged with helping the formerly enslaved, many feel that contracts it helped to negotiate were part of the creation of the sharecropping system. At the same time, the Freedmen's Bureau was an impetus for the development of many HBCUs.

From emancipation, formerly enslaved people attempted to amass capital and play a role in our nation's economy. Congress chartered the Freedman's Saving and Trust Company in 1865. By 1874, deposits totaled more than $3 million, but the bank had been so poorly run that when the abolitionist Frederick Douglass became its president in 1874, he declared it bankrupt. Though Congress chartered this bank, it refused to reimburse depositors (in contrast to the profligate bailout of 2008). Historians Mary Frances Berry and John Blassingame say this bank's failure "created a deep suspicion of all financial institutions in the black community and contributed to the development of spendthrift attitudes which long afterward plagued blacks."

Against all odds, African-Americans also began to acquire land. By 1910, African-American people had more than 15 million acres of rural land, but Black farms were smaller and less well capitalized than White farms – a prescription for land loss during the 20th century. By 1999, Black rural land ownership had dropped to 7.7 million acres, or just 1 percent of all privately owned rural land in the United States. Much of this land loss was a function of the deliberate exploitation of African-American landowners. In 2001, the Associated Press released a series of articles called "Torn from the Land" which documented the history of African-American land loss in the South. The research, from more than 1000 interviews and public records, found 107 documented land takings in 13 southern and border states. [7] More than half of these takings were violent, and others involved fraud, trickery, and legal exploitation. Documentation of government discrimination by the Department of Agriculture in its disparate efforts to assist Black and White farmers suggests the playing field in landownership remains uneven. At the same time, it is important to note the passionate quest for land that many African-Americans had, and the role land ownership played in Black economic development.

In the same ways that African-Americans were separated from our land, so were we separated from our property and economic successes. Racism spurred a vicious economic envy that often erupted in violence when successful African-Americans were not sufficiently subservient to less successful Whites. In Wilmington, North Carolina, for example, economic envy incited Whites to destroy a thriving Black community on November 10, 1898. The Black newspaper was burned, dozens of African-American citizens were murdered, and some of the wealthiest and most successful African-Americans and their White allies were banned from the city. Thomas C. Miller, worth more than 30,000 1898 dollars (the equivalent of more than a million of today's dollars) was one of those exiled. He was never able to make an economic comeback.

Similarly, on June 1, 1921, Tulsa, Oklahoma's Black Wall Street, a prospering African-American community, was burned to the ground by mobs of envious Whites and even bombed from the air. In just 12 hours, a vibrant Black business district was transformed into smoldering rubble, with most of the Black citizens of that town fenced into a virtual concentration camp, their businesses gone, their homes burned or looted. To this day, there is no accurate count of the number of lives lost in the evisceration of Black Wall Street. [8]

Despite the violent consequences of African-American economic participation and success, African-Americans "kept on keeping on," attempting, against all odds, to start businesses, buy homes, and start unions and professional organizations when excluded from majority organizations. As our nation embarked on an industrial revolution that empowered some laborers, African-Americans were used by White industrialists as strike-breakers to suppress union wages. This should have been a moment when Black and White labor joined to increase wages in both communities, but the forces of racism were often stronger than the forces of class solidarity. The United Mine Workers were an exception to the general rule of union exclusion in the early twentieth century. In tribute to the collective flexing of Black economic power, A. Philip Randolph was notably successful in organizing 9000 Pullman porters in 1925, and in receiving a charter from the Associated Federation of Laborers (AFL). Because he had an AFL charter, A Philip Randolph, a passionate advocate for desegregation, became a thorn in the side of organized labor.

We kept on keeping on. Even as thriving communities were destroyed and millions were quasi-enslaved through sharecropping, entrepreneurial African-Americans dared develop economic vehicles and amass wealth. Maggie Lena Walker of Richmond Virginia was the first woman to found a bank in the United States. Born in 1867 to former slaves, Walker had been active in the Grand United Order of St. Luke, an African-American cooperative insurance society. She became secretary-treasurer of the organization in 1899, and opened the St. Luke Penny Savings Bank in 1903 with less than $10,000 in deposits. By 1920, the bank had helped more than 600 African-American families to purchase homes. By 1924, it had 50,000 members, a staff of 50 in its Richmond headquarters, and assets of almost $400,000. Though many Black banks did not survive the Great Depression, Walker's did. She merged her institution with two smaller Black banks in 1930. [9] It was reorganized as Consolidated Bank and Trust and existed until it recently fell victim to the Great Recession. As of September 2010, Consolidated Bank and Trust will be merged with several other banks, but its legacy will not be swallowed by history as long as we remain inspired by the financial acumen of its founder, Maggie Lena Walker.

Maggie Lena Walker was among dozens of African-American pioneers who founded financial institutions – banks, insurance companies, and trade associations – to provide access to those who were relegated to the periphery by the segregation of the post-slavery era. North Carolina Mutual Life Insurance Company was founded in 1898, and it is the oldest and largest African-American life insurance company in the United States. Modeled after the mutual benefit societies that assisted African-Americans in the early 19th century, North Carolina Mutual has been a catalyst for minority social and economic development. The organization continues to thrive in Durham, North Carolina. Financial institutions like Consolidated Bank and Trust and North Carolina Mutual Life Insurance Co. were available to African-American people when other financial organizations denied them access. Although many institutions did not survive, it is important to note that African-Americans organized 134 banks between 1888 and 1934.

Even as financial institutions were being established, African-American entrepreneurs were developing institutions that provided employment opportunities for those whom others might not employ. Madame C.J. Walker is perhaps the most noted African-American entrepreneur of the early twentieth century. Madame, as she was known, parlayed her knowledge of herbs that enhanced hair growth and turned that into a thriving business that made her a philanthropist, civil rights activist, and our nation's first Black woman millionaire. Her generosity to organizations like the NAACP and her patronage of the arts are legendary, but her most important contribution may have been the development of a thriving business that, at its peak, had thousands of employees and independent sales agents. [10]

While she may have been among the largest and most visible of African-American entrepreneurs, she was part of a cadre of thousands who started businesses. Most of these businesses were, as they are today, sole proprietorships (today, 85 percent of Black-owned businesses are one-owner operations). Still, against a backdrop of segregation and oppression, Black people operated 25,000 businesses in 1929 with revenues of $101 million. By 1939, there were more businesses – 30,000 – but less revenue ($71.5 million). The number of Black-owned businesses declined in the 1950s, and by 1960, African-Americans were just 2.5 percent of self-employed business owners in the U. S. The number has risen only slightly, with African-Americans representing fewer than 4 percent of self-employed owners today. Under segregation, many African-American businesses experienced both advantages and disadvantages. While majority businesses did not compete for African-American customers, many African-American entrepreneurs did not have access to the capital provided by majority banks. With fewer reserves, African-American entrepreneurs were often more vulnerable to market fluctuations and the predatory practices of majority business owners.

An African-American collective consciousness developed during segregation, partly nurtured by the Negro Business League founded by Booker T. Washington, partly by African-American civic organizations, and partly by the Black press which served as both an economic engine and "the talking drum" for African-American communities. The Black press carried the philosophies of Marcus Garvey, A. Philip Randolph, and W.E.B. Du Bois to the community. The press publicized the "Don't Buy Where You Can't Work" campaigns that urged African-Americans to picket stores in Harlem that exploited, but failed to hire, African-Americans. At the peak of activity in 1956, there were about 350 Black-owned newspapers. *Ebony* and *Jet* magazines were established during the period of segregation by Johnson Publishing Company, a multi-media conglomerate that continues to thrive. The publishing business was precarious during segregation; it is even more so today, as consolidation continues to swallow vehicles (such as *Essence* magazine) that were formerly Black-owned. Will "the drum" beat a message of community connection with fewer vehicles, and with hands that aren't completely connected to our community?

African-Americans made inroads in academia and government service during the one hundred years between slavery and civil rights. Dr. Sadie Tanner Mossell Alexander was the first African-American woman to earn a Ph.D. in Economics in 1921, with a dissertation based on studies of one of the pivotal economic movements of her era, The Great Migration, in which millions of African-Americans left the South for the North. "The Migration of the Negro to Philadelphia: 1916-1919" is a masterful study of the impact of migration on the city of Philadelphia, highlighting ways that housing segregation shaped socio-political relationships in the African-American community, and analyzing how redlining affected consumption. Dr. Alexander studied African-American migration, consumption, and social relations in a dissertation that "withstands the test of time" as a still-readable and laudable document. After earning her doctorate, she earned a law degree, married and had two children, practiced law, and became an active civic leader (and first National President of Delta Sigma Theta Sorority, Incorporated). She served on the boards of the National Urban League and the United Nations Association, traveled internationally, and served on several presidential commissions. Her work in economics is often eclipsed by her subsequent accomplishments, but her contribution to Black Economic History is undeniable.

In government service, President Franklin D. Roosevelt developed a Black "kitchen cabinet" that included people like Mary McLeod Bethune and Robert Weaver, the latter eventually becoming secretary of the Department of Housing and Urban Development under President Lyndon B. Johnson. Advisors such as Bethune and Weaver frequently influenced presidents in their position on Black economic development, including their support of desegregation and workforce improvement efforts.

Still, the Great Depression had a series of recovery efforts that often sidelined African-Americans, or included them on a delayed basis. And the economic expansion that came from wartime work efforts during World War II only slowly included African- Americans. African-American unemployment remained high during the Second World War, and in some cases, defense contractors imported White workers to southern locations rather than employing African-Americans. When A. Philip Randolph threatened to stage a March on Washington in

INTRODUCTION_____

1941 because of discrimination in defense employment, President Roosevelt issued Executive Order 8802 banning discrimination and creating the Fair Employment Practices Commission.

Racial economic injustice was exacerbated by the GI Bill and other policies that, while advantaging veterans, often explicitly disadvantaged African-Americans. In his book, *When Affirmative Action Was White,* [11] the historian Ira Katznelson describes the series of domestic programs through which the federal government transferred billions of dollars to create housing, jobs, business development, and educational and retirement opportunities for Whites, but not for Blacks. As an example, veteran's benefits were decreed by national legislation, but they were administered locally. In the South, hostility to African-American veterans resulted in limited access to the loans and other benefits that all taxpayers had subsidized. Thus, according to Katznelson, of 3229 GI Bill – guaranteed home, business, and farm loans made in Mississippi in 1947, only two were granted to African-American veterans. This "twisted and unstated" form of White affirmative action has been instrumental in widening the racial economic gap. Those who scoff at the notion of reparations, or chide African-Americans for dependence on "government handouts" might look at what it cost to provide the foundations of White middle class status, and quantify how different things might be if African-Americans had the opportunity to participate equally in the government programs that transferred billions of dollars to Whites between 1945 and 1955.

The 1865-1964 period of legal segregation had an oscillating rhythm of setback and success. Structurally and institutionally, African-Americans were consistently challenged by a playing field that was not level, and despite that, there were many successes. Patents were obtained, businesses were started, college educations were completed, and communities were developed by Blacks in this period. The role of the church and of civil rights and community organizations was developed and strengthened to the point that these organizations were able to challenge the basic tenets of segregation in a series of stunning court actions that included Brown v. Board of Education. These institutions also led the way in collective street actions that included non-violent protests and the Montgomery Bus Boycott, a moment in both civil rights and economic history. The 1963 March on Washington was a march for civil rights, but Dr. King infused it with economic content when he thundered, "We have come to the nation's capital to cash a check," adding, "America has given the Negro people a bad check; a check which has come back marked 'Insufficient funds.'" [12] Our civil rights history and our economic history are powerfully connected, as exemplified by that statement.

Surviving and Thriving After The Passage of the Civil Rights Act of 1964

The passage of the Civil Rights Act of 1964 effectively ended legal segregation. However, nearly fifty years after the passage of the Civil Rights Act, vestiges of segregation and discrimination still exist. Witness, for example, the discriminatory treatment of African-American farmers by the Department of Agriculture, and the failure, by the summer of 2010, for Congress to authorize compensation for these farmers although wrong-doing has been acknowledged. Consider the number of racial discrimination cases still heard by the Equal Employment Opportunity Commission (EEOC), and cases that are not heard because many companies are not transparent about pay differentials and other forms of discrimination. The passage of the Civil Rights Act did not level the economic playing field, but it did open doors and provide opportunities in education, employment, and economic development.

An immediate consequence of the Civil Rights Act of 1964 was the formation of the Equal Employment Opportunity Commission, which conducted a series of investigations into the unequal treatment of African-Americans and women in the workplace. Dr. Phyllis Ann Wallace, the first African-American woman to receive the Ph.D. in Economics from Yale University, became the first research director of the EEOC. Her work was instrumental in illustrating patterns of discrimination against African-Americans and in making more opportunities available in both manufacturing and Corporate America. The 1964-1968 period was tense and confrontational, with extremely slow progress and significant resistance to the Civil Rights Act. At the same time, this was also a period of firsts, with a few African-Americans being hired in jobs from which we had heretofore been excluded. Some universities opened their doors to African-Americans for the first time, as did some workplaces. It did not hurt that President Lyndon B. Johnson's Great Society programs were implemented during these years. However, the pressure to make more rapid progress was accelerated by the assassination of Dr. Martin Luther King, Jr. in 1968.

President Richard Nixon established the Minority Business Development Agency (originally the Office of Minority Business Enterprise) in 1969. Part of his Executive Order reads, "The opportunity for full participation in our free enterprise system by socially and economically disadvantaged persons is essential if we are to obtain social and economic justice for such persons and improve the functioning of our national economy." It is fascinating that such a conservative President freely used terms like "economic justice" to rationalize the creation of a federal program that would assist minorities in wealth development. The concept of "economic justice" is often scorned in contemporary times and, indeed, sometimes described as "class warfare." In any case, the Minority Business Development Agency was at least somewhat responsible for increasing African-American business presence, although critics of Nixon's "Black Capitalism" movement saw it as a cynical ploy to attract minority voters to the Republican Party.

Black Enterprise magazine was founded in this era, as was *Essence* magazine. Atlanta Mayor Maynard Jackson used his office to ensure that African-American entrepreneurs had access to city contracts, indicating that majority contracts could "subcontract, or no contract" to share the wealth. In hundreds of other cities, minority business set-asides created new contracting opportunities for African-American and other minority entrepreneurs.

The Civil Rights Act of 1964 was supplemented by the Equal Employment Act of 1972 which gave the EEOC enforcement powers, authorizing it to call for the cancellation of federal contracts awarded to those who discriminated. However, enforcement powers were only rarely used, and few government contracts were cancelled. According to Mary Frances Berry and John Blassingame, less than one tenth of one percent of the federal budget was devoted to ending discrimination in 1975. [13] The U.S. Commission on Civil Rights observed that enforcement of civil rights laws was so lax that the laws were "practically meaningless." After just a decade of affirmative action, a "reverse discrimination case," Bakke v. University of California, had a "chilling effect" on the affirmative action process.

Despite tepid anti-discrimination legislation, and frequent legal attacks on Black economic and employment progress, the 1964-1980 period was, in some ways, a heady time in that the race conversation, once whispered, gained volume. The Black Panther Party gained traction among young African-Americans because of its position of "self-determination." There was an increase in the formation of Black professional advocacy organizations that focused both on dealing with challenges in the African-American community and demanding a fair share of jobs and opportunities from Corporate America. Such organizations included the Council of Black Economists (now the National Economics Association), the National Association of Black Accountants (founded in 1970), the National Black MBA Association, the Black American Law Students Association (BALSA), and other groups which used race and professional affiliation as their organizing principles. The traditional civil rights associations were also often challenged by newer, more militant organizations that were more vocal in their demands for jobs and justice.

Robert S. Browne founded the Black Economic Research Center (BERC) in 1969. His work was partly funded by foundations, highlighting the role the foundation sector often played in the research and exploration of issues of economic justice. Philanthropic involvement in the African-American community did not begin in the years after the passage of the Civil Rights Act, though it may have increased at this time. Still, foundation involvement in organizations like BERC depended on the ability of Black leaders to make a compelling case for their existence.

Even as African-Americans were recognized as a socio-political force, they were also recognized as a consumer market. D. Parke Gibson authored *The $30 Billion Negro* in 1969, [14] and talked about ways that corporations could gain by targeting advertising and opportunities to African-Americans. Gibson followed this book with $70 Billion in the Black in 1978. [15] Today, the book might be titled *The $900 Billion Dollar African-American,* based on the current income of African-American people. The Black consumer has become a consumer to be courted, even as Black advertising agencies are disappearing because larger ad agencies have developed expertise in marketing to African-Americans.

Indeed, twenty-first century "post-racial" multiculturalism has challenged Black economic development in many ways. Even in the face of continuing racial economic inequality, there are those who feel that race-specific organizations, foci, or remedies are unnecessary. At the same time, and using subtle language, those who feel this way often discriminate. For example, the hardest working man in radio, Tom Joyner, exposed the ugliness of the "non-urban dictate" some companies imposed on advertising agencies. Simply translated, a non-urban dictate means: "We don't want African-American business." How's that for contemporary discrimination?

However, it is important to note the extent to which African-American networking and "empowerment" opportunities have significant corporate sponsorship. A review of the sponsors of events like the Essence Music Festival, Tavis Smiley's annual (2000-2010) State of the Black Union gatherings, and the Congressional Black Caucus Foundation's Annual Legislative Forum activities suggest that networking and access are enhanced by corporate relationships. On one hand, corporate sponsorship speaks to the power of African-American consumers and the necessity and desirability of courting this market. On the other hand, how free are those who accept corporate sponsorship to craft a message that is empowering? (Full disclosure: I've participated in all of these events.)

An assessment of African-American progress in the years since the passage of the Civil Rights Act is as challenging as the experience of oscillating progress has been for us in this era. Is the glass half empty or half full? From an aggregate perspective, African-Americans are much better off than we were when the Civil Rights Act was passed, though at the same time it must be stated that certain metrics have not changed significantly. For example, Black unemployment is still nearly twice White unemployment. And, despite the growth of the Black middle class, disproportionate poverty and its persistence plagues the African-American community. No one would wish to roll back the clock, to return to a time when African-American people were oppressed by abject segregation. Nonetheless, it is possible to look at Black middle class progress and overstate gains. Does the election of an African-American President, for example, obviate the need to close racial economic gaps?

While the playing field is not yet level (and you can't win the game when one player has loaded dice, as Berry and Blassingame suggest), there remain occasions of celebration. Those few African-Americans who have led Fortune 500 companies, including Time Warner's Dick Parsons, American Express's Ken Chenault, Fannie Mae's Franklin Raines, and Xerox's Ursula Burns, among others, are a testament to progress. Lisa Price, the owner of Carol's Daughter, comes to us in the spirit of Madame C.J. Walker, Fashion Fair Cosmetics, and others who made the search for beauty a foundation of entrepreneurial success. Similarly, the Cathy Liggins Hughes story – of a woman who felt so strongly about her vision that she slept in her radio station for a time to pay her broadcasting bills instead of rent – reminds us of the tenacity that entrepreneurship requires. Perhaps the most stunning entrepreneurial story of the late 20th century is that of Robert L. Johnson, the founder (with Sheila Johnson) of Black Entertainment Television, the company that was sold to Viacom for about $3 billion. Several senior executives at BET also achieved multi-millionaire status as a result of this sale.

The purpose of this book, *Surviving and Thriving: 365 Facts in Black Economic History,* is to highlight Black economic success in the face of persistent challenges, and to inspire and encourage all of us to be players, and winners, in our nation's economic system. To be sure, the dice are loaded, the game is rigged, and absent reparations, African-Americans will never "catch up." Still, if we don't fully commit to playing the game, the gap is likely to widen even more. The game is not just a game of starting or owning a business or leading a large corporation. Part of the contest is the game of signifying, protesting, and calling out the forces of oppression that result in racial economic gaps. Thus, it is important that Black farmers are made whole. It is important that dollars spent on economic recovery are more evenly distributed. It is important that the achievement gap (which partly leads to the racial economic gap) be closed. Even as we achieve, we must protest inequality and its foundations.

The conflict between participating in a rigged capitalist system and protesting it has been the central tension in my life as an activist and economist. I always want to enthusiastically applaud African-American progress, and especially lift up those who achieve against the odds. At the same time, I want the African-American community and others to understand both the implicit unfairness in our rigged system and the need to protest and develop public policy to make the system fairer. I have dreamed of producing these Black Economic History facts for two decades, realizing that role models can come from anywhere, and that the symbol of a slave purchasing herself speaks an enormous faith and commitment to freedom, even in the face of unfairness. Anyone who experiences economic unfairness – higher interest or unemployment rates, for example – ought to get inspiration from Free Frank, Elizabeth Keckley, and John Parker. If they can prevail, so can we.

Our economy is rigged to widen the racial economic gap. Our resistance can narrow the gap. Our Black economic history is a history of resistance. It is a rich history of making a difference even when we were written off. African-American people cannot accept the

INTRODUCTION_____

peripheral status that many have assigned to us. When obstacles were greater than they are today, we were persistent in elbowing our way into the rigged game. Can we do any less now?

In her poem, "And Still I Rise," Dr. Maya Angelou wrote, "You can write me down in history with your bitter, twisted lies, you can trod me in the very dirt and still, like dust, I rise." More than a century before she penned her words, Richard R. Wright, Sr., a man born into slavery who rose to lofty heights as a school founder, educator, newspaper publisher, entrepreneur, political organizer, banker, and scholar, asked General Oliver Otis Howard to "Tell them we are rising." Wright's nineteenth-century vision that the combination of education and the acquisition of economic and political power would propel African-Americans to success has currency today. Tell them we are rising, surviving, and thriving. Tell anyone who will listen that, while the playing field is not yet level, African-American people can play the game, win it, and even change the rules to make them fairer. Tell them we are rising. While the facts included in this book are not exhaustive, they should inspire and tickle our imaginations. Tell them we are rising; tell them our Black Economic History.

NOTES

1. Income and poverty data are found in "Income Poverty and Health Insurance Coverage in the United States," US Government Printing Office, P60-236, Washington, DC 2009; employment data at www.bls.gov ("The Employment Situation," US Government Printing Office, Washington, DC 20090, USDL-10-1212).

2. Debbie Gruenstein Bocian, et al., "Foreclosures by Race and Ethnicity: The Demographics of a Crisis," Center for Responsible Lending, June, 2010.

3. John Parker, *His Promised Land: The Autobiography of John P. Parker, Former Slave and Conductor on the Underground Railroad* (edited by Stuart Seely Sprague), New York: Norton, 1986.

4. Juliet Walker, *Free Frank: A Black Pioneer on the Antebellum Frontier,* University Press of Kentucky, 1995.

5. Colin A. Palmer, *Passageways: An Interpretive History of Black America* Belmont, CA: Wadsorth Group, 2002, p. 187.

6. Melvin R. Williams, *A Statistical Study of Blacks in Washington, DC in 1860,* Washington, DC: Columbia Historical Society, 1980.

7. Todd Lewan and Delores Barclay, "Torn From the Land: Black Americans' Farmland Taken Through Cheating, Intimidation, Even Murder," Associated Press, December 2001.

8. Tim Madigan, *The Burning: Massacre, Destruction and the Tulsa Race Riot of 1921,* New York: St. Martin's Press, 2003.

NOTES

9. Gertrude Woodruff Marlow, *Right Worthy Grand Mission? Maggie Lena Walker and the Quest for Black Economic Empowerment,* Washington, DC: Howard University Press, 2003.

10. ALelia Bundles, *On Her Own Ground: The Life and Times of Madam C.J. Walker,* New York: Scribner, 2002.

11. Ira Katznelson, *When Affirmative Action Was White: An Untold History of Racial Inequality in Twentieth Century America,* New York: W. W. Norton and Company, 2006.

12. Martin Luther King, Jr., "I Have A Dream," Washington, DC, 1963.

13. Mary Frances Berry and John W. Blassingame, *Long Memory: The Black Experience in America,* Chapter 6, "The Economics of Hope and Despair", New York: Oxford University Press, 1982.

14. D. Parke Gibson, *The $30 Billion Negro,* New York: McMillan Publishing, 1969.

15. D. Parke Gibson, *$70 Billion in the Black: America's Black Consumers,* New York: McMillan Publishing, 1978.

SURVIVING
AND THRIVING
365 *facts*
IN BLACK ECONOMIC HISTORY

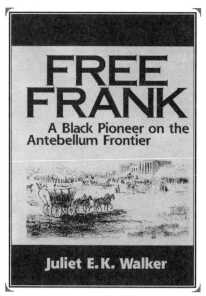

University Press of Kentucky

Free Frank McWorter

(1836)

Free Frank McWorter founded New Philadelphia, Illinois in 1836 and the town was platted in 1840. He was the first African-American to be the founder of a town. He earned money for the land by establishing an extractive mining operation while he was still enslaved. McWorter, known as Free Frank because he had purchased his own freedom, owned property valued at $2,694; his real property, 560 acres, was valued at $2,320 and his personal property at $374. With the money Free Frank earned by selling town lots and other business opportunities, he eventually purchased freedom for 16 family members. In contrast to some all-Black towns founded after the Civil War where Blacks purchased town lots from Whites, Whites actually purchased New Philadelphia town lots from Free Frank.

Benjamin Carr

(1862)

Benjamin Carr, born in 1862, did farm work for $30 a year before acquiring a small tract of land for $100. Three decades later he owned a 400-acre farm near Hartsville, TN complete with pastures, fruit orchards, and herds of livestock. In 1909, Carr was one of the speakers at the National Negro Business League meeting at Louisville, KY, delivering the address "Succeeding as a Farmer."

Lewis Temple

(1848)

In 1848, Lewis Temple invented the Temple's Toggle or Temple's Iron. It was the state-of-the-art whaling harpoon of its time. Temple sold his harpoon and other whale craft in a shop in New Bedford, Massachusetts. Experts acknowledge that Temple's harpoon was "the single most important invention in the whole history of whaling."

Savannah Wharf Workers' Strike

(1891)

Demanding union recognition, overtime pay, and a promise that employers provide fair wages, the Savannah Wharf Workers' Strike began in 1891 when over 1,500 Black longshoremen walked off their jobs. Although their numbers later increased to over 2,500, after job threats and low morale the leaders eventually called off the strike.

Frederick Massiah

(1886)

Frederick Massiah was born in 1886. Massiah was an engineer and entrepreneur who started his own construction company at a time when African-Americans often encountered significant difficulty securing financing, insurance, and trade union acceptance. Marsh was one of the first African-Americans to flourish as a contracting engineer. His numerous projects included the William Donner X-Ray Laboratory at the University of Pennsylvania and the Sewage Disposal Plant in Trenton, New Jersey. Marsh made advancements in the use of concrete prior to their incorporation into prevalent building codes. He received the Harmon Foundation Medal for Engineering in recognition for his contributions.

Anna T. Jeanes

(1907)

The Anna T. Jeanes Fund began in 1907. Jeanes, a Quaker philanthropist, donated money from 1905 to 1907 for the fund's establishment. The monies were used to provide aid to rural schools for African-Americans in the South and to furnish special instructors in the industrial arts and extension work.

| 3 |

Elizabeth Keckley

(1860)

Primarily known as Mary Todd Lincoln's dressmaker, Elizabeth Keckley also owned the largest custom dressmaking business in Washington, DC. She moved to the city in 1860 and quickly became its most sought after modiste. In addition to making clothing for the first lady, she designed dresses for the wives of Jefferson Davis and Robert E. Lee. Because of her semi-celebrity status, Keckley used her connections to create the Contraband Relief Association, a non-profit organization that helped disadvantaged African-Americans. Keckley's autobiography was entitled *Behind the Scenes or, Thirty Years a Slave and Four Years in the White House.*

San Francisco History Center, San Francisco Public Library.

Mary Ellen Pleasant

(1852)

California's Slave Act forced Mary Ellen Pleasant to assume two identities in order to avoid capture when she arrived in San Francisco in 1852. At this time, anyone without freedom papers could be sent back into slavery. Her two identities: 'Mrs. Ellen Smith,' a White boardinghouse cook serving the wealthiest and most influential men while leveraging secrets for favors such as providing jobs and privileges for Colored people; and 'Mrs. Pleasant,' an abolitionist-turned-entrepreneur who used her money to help ex-slaves fight the California Slave Act and become business owners. Pleasant's fortune was once assessed at $30 million.

Henry H. Brown

(1990)

In 1990, Henry H. Brown became the first African-American to serve as a Senior Executive in the Anheuser-Busch company when he was elected to the position of Senior Vice-President. Brown's contributions to the organization include the development of Budweiser's "Great Kings and Queens of Africa" program. The program was created to make the rich ancestral history and traditions of African-Americans more widely known.

John Somerville

(1882)

John Somerville was the first African-American member of the Los Angeles Chamber of Commerce. Born in 1882, Somerville immigrated to San Francisco, California from Jamaica. Initially working in a bowling alley, Somerville saved his wages and in two years was able to enroll in the University of Southern California School of Dentistry. He would later marry fellow alumni Vada Watson. Watson was the first African-American woman, and second African-American, to graduate from the University's dental school. Somerville founded the Los Angeles chapter of the NAACP and, with his wife, built a 26-unit apartment building named the La Vada.

Aulana L. Peters

(1984)
_____

The first African-American and third woman to serve as commissioner for the Securities and Exchange Commission (SEC) was Aulana L. Peters in 1984. She served in this capacity until 1988. The SEC is an independent government agency charged with regulating the securities industry.

Lewis Winter

(1889)
_____

In 1889, Lewis Winter was described as the richest Negro in the state of Tennessee. When Winter arrived in Nashville, he began his business with only $40. Winter, a freedman, sold eggs and poultry and held real estate valued at $70,000. His business became the largest of its kind in the South, with Winter shipping sixty-five boxcar loads of poultry and produce to buyers in New York and Philadelphia in a six-month period.

Valerie Daniels-Carter

(1984)
_____

Valerie Daniels-Carter is president and chief executive officer of the largest African-American—owned restaurant franchise: V & J Holding Companies, Inc. Her dream began in 1984 when she opened her first Burger King restaurant in Milwaukee. Under the helm of Daniels-Carter, the Milwaukee, Wisconsin-based corporation operates more than 100 Pizza Huts and Burger Kings in four states. *Black Enterprise* listed it as one of the top 100 Industrial/Service companies with sales of over $97 million in 2006.

| 5 |

Stephen Smith

(1840)
_____

Stephen Smith started a successful lumber and coal business. He also owned about fifty houses in Philadelphia and more in Lancaster and Columbia, Pennsylvania in the 1840s. By 1864, Smith was worth $500,000 and was one of the wealthiest Black men in the United States before the Civil War.

Courtesy of Library of Congress Prints and Photographs Division, Washington, DC.

Town of Nicodemus

(1878) African-American settlers from Kentucky arrived in Kansas to establish the Town of Nicodemus in 1878. It became the first of hundreds of all-Black or predominately-Black western towns. Nicodemus was planned in 1877 by W.R. Hill, a land developer from Indiana, and Reverend W.H. Smith, a Black man, who worked together to form the Nicodemus Town Company. The Reverend Simon P. Roundtree was the first settler, arriving on June 18, 1877. Zack T. Fletcher and his wife, Jenny Smith Fletcher (the daughter of Reverend W.H. Smith), arrived in July and Fletcher was named Secretary of the Town Company. Smith, Roundtree, and the Fletchers made claims to their property and built temporary homes in dugouts along the prairie.

Franklin D. Raines

(1985) Franklin D. Raines was named a general partner of Lazard Freres and Co. in 1985. He was the first African-American to become a partner at a majority-owned global investment bank. Raines served as the Director of the Office of Management and Budget under President Bill Clinton from 1996-1998. Later, Raines achieved another first when he became CEO of Fannie Mae.

Jerome Holland

(1972) Jerome Holland became the first African-American in 1972 to sit on the board of the New York Stock Exchange, and he did so until 1980. Holland also wrote a number of economic studies of African-Americans, including "Black Opportunity 1969."

James Guilford, Jr.

(1911)

In 1911, James Guilford, Jr. was the first African-American president of the Associated Master Barbers of Massachusetts. Guilford established and operated Dunbar Barbers from 1934 until 1942. He was also owner and proprietor of Jimmy Guilford's Men's Hairstyling Salon from 1945 until 1979.

Herman Roberts

(1960)

Herman Roberts is one of the foremost African-American hoteliers in the country. The Beggs, Oklahoma native opened his first Roberts Motel in 1960 in Chicago, Illinois. Ten years later, he opened his sixth property, which remains his most well-known. A Chicago landmark, the sixth hotel is the first fully-equipped Black-owned motel in the nation and boasts 250 guest rooms, 2 penthouse party suites, a restaurant, lounge, ballroom, travel agency, and convenience store. Herman was an early entrepreneur, by age 12 he was shining shoes, delivering newspapers, and doing many other odd jobs. When Herman was 18 he had saved enough money to purchase his own taxi and license. By 1944, he had established the Roberts Cab Company.

Oscar Howard

(1956)

Oscar Howard operated a food service business in the Twin Cities arsenal near Minneapolis, Minnesota during the Korean War. In 1956, Howard opened Howard Catering Company. In the mid 1960s, Howard took part in the War on Poverty, a program that provided home-delivered meals to elderly residents. He later started a non-profit minority entrepreneurial program called the Metropolitan Economic Development Association (MEDA).

| 7 |

William A. Leidesdorff

(1841)

In 1841, William A. Leidesdorff piloted the schooner, Julia Ann, from Boston to Yerba Buena — a Mexican village that was later renamed San Francisco. A pioneer of the Golden State, Leidesdorff was the first African-American Consul, and held the position of treasurer of the city of San Francisco. He was a successful merchant, and he routinely made trips from his home state of California to both Mexico and Hawaii. Leidesdorff also launched many businesses, including the first steamboat in the San Francisco Bay.

Courtesy of Library of Congress Prints and Photographs Division, Washington, DC.

Normal School for Colored Teachers (Tuskegee Institute)

(1881) In 1881, the Normal School for Colored Teachers opened in Tuskegee, Alabama. The school's founding is credited to Lewis Adams, a former slave who suggested the idea for the agricultural school. Booker T. Washington was named the school's first principal and ultimately chosen to head the school. Washington brought the best African-American professionals to join him at the school. Botanist George Washington Carver, Robert Taylor, the first Black architect to graduate from the Massachusetts Institute of Technology, and David A. Williston, one of the first Black landscape architects in America, were faculty members. The school became the nucleus of Tuskegee Institute and was located on the site of Tuskegee University's present campus.

Thomas J. Burrell

(1971) Known for creating positive and upbeat advertisements, Burrell Communications, founded by Thomas J. Burrell in 1971. In 1978, 1985 and 1986 Burrell received the Clio Award – the highest honor in the advertising industry. Burrell Communications has won many other awards for its ads. As a writer, Burrell authored *Brainwashed: Challenging the Myth of Black Inferiority* in 2010.

Francis Cardozo

(1868) Francis Cardozo was the first African-American to serve as a Cabinet officer in state government. As Secretary of State of South Carolina (1868), he was instrumental in reforming the South Carolina Land Commission, which facilitated the distribution of land to former slaves. He was reelected as secretary of state in 1870. Additionally, he served as Treasurer of South Carolina from 1872 until 1876. In 1877, Cardozo left South Carolina, accepting a post in the U.S. Treasury Department in Washington, DC.

Ernest P. Joshua

(1970)

The J.M Company was established by Ernest P. Joshua in 1970, and the company later became known as J.M. Products, Inc. – a major minority-owned and operated aerosol manufacturing company. J.M. Products' best known item was Isoplus, a spray created and designed to combat hair thinning as a result of perms and other chemical processes.

Nail and Parker Associates

(1909)

In 1909, Henry Parker and John Nail created Nail and Parker Associates in anticipation of the Great Migration's potential to increase the population of New York. The New York-based realty company counseled middle-class African-Americans to purchase available property in Harlem, as well as providing mortgages by purchasing, appraising managing, and selling properties. Nail, who served as president, made the argument that buying property would undermine discriminatory practices toward African-Americans in real estate. One of Nail and Parker's customers was Madame C.J. Walker, who bought $200.000 worth of properties.

James C. Napier

(1845)

Born in 1845, James C. Napier, a lawyer, businessman, and politician, was the first African-American to serve on the Nashville City Council. He was instrumental in hiring Black teachers for Colored public schools. In addition, he hired Black detectives and organized the Black Fire-engine Company during the 1880's. Napier served as President of the National Negro Business League. He also founded the One Cent Bank in 1904. The One Cent Bank is now known as Citizens Savings Bank.

| 9 |

Frank Ferrell

(1886)

In 1886, trade unionist Frank Ferrell represented his Richmond organization in the Knights of Labor's (KOL) General Assembly, and was given the opportunity to introduce Grand Master Workman Terence V. Powderly, who then introduced the governor. Because of his race, Ferrell wasn't allowed to stay in the same hotel as other delegates. Nearly one hundred White delegates rallied to support him, and Powderly discussed the need for racial equality in the labor movement, creating an environment where African-Americans were seen as equals in a traditionally all-White labor union for the first time.

Courtesy of Library of Congress Prints and Photographs Division, Washington, DC.

Mound Bayou

(1887) In 1887, cousins Isaiah T. Montgomery and Benjamin Green founded the town of Mound Bayou, Mississippi. Mound Bayou was one of the first incorporated Black Towns in the United States. The buyers purchased the land from a plantation owner with the goal of organizing a community composed exclusively of Colored people. Montgomery had all of the land titled in his name. The land was rented to tenants for a $0.50 per acre entrance fee. Much of the town's economic growth and pride stemmed from its development of the nation's only Black-owned cottonseed mill, along with a railroad station, a bank, a smokehouse, a sawmill, a gin, a dock, and other businesses. Mound Bayou was called "The Jewel of the Delta."

Fannie B. Peck

(1933) Fannie B. Peck founded the Housewives League of Detroit (HLD). Based on the theory that housewives controlled approximately 80% of their family's income, HLD designed a consumer-based support model that improved the economic condition of African-Americans in Detroit, Michigan. Other cities organized their own Housewives Leagues. In 1933, these leagues came together as the Housewives League of America. Fannie B. Peck served as President.

Henry E. Parker

(1975) Henry E. Parker became the second African-American to hold the Connecticut's state treasurer's office from 1975 to 1986. Parker was responsible for shrinking the state's $149 million pension investment fund loss to a number around $34 million in 1978. Parker reorganized Connecticut's investment portfolio to include two-thirds bonds and enabled Black firms to manage a significant portion of the $800 million pension fund.

Rose Meta House of Beauty, Inc.

(1950)

By 1950, the Rose Meta House of Beauty was the largest African-American-owned chain of beauty salons in the nation, boasting revenue in excess of $3 million. Born in 1912, Morgan also helped found Freedom National Bank, the only African-American-owned commercial bank in New York.

Maria W. Stewart

(1833)

Maria W. Stewart criticized African-American men for failing to move towards self-improvement and not fighting for equal rights. In her 1833 speech titled, "On African Rights and Liberty," not only did Stewart defend her own right to speak publicly, but she also criticized the colonization movement's plans to send African-Americans back to Africa. Noting the situations of the time – Whites stealing land from Native Americans, and stealing Africans from their own land to become slaves – Stewart argued that Blacks should fight and gain more legal and economic freedom in the United States instead of returning to Africa.

George Grant

(1899)

In 1899, George Grant patented the first golf tee. Grant's innovative design is the basis for the wooden tees of today. Though the U.S. Patent Office in Boston granted him the patent, the United States Golf Association would not recognize Grant's significant contribution until 1991, nearly 100 years later. When not golfing, Grant was also a prominent local dentist. He was the second African-American to graduate from Harvard Dental School and one of the first African-American dentists to practice in the United States.

Norbert Rillieux

(1846)

Norbert Rillieux, born in 1846, was an African-American chemist and engineer who revolutionized the sugar refining process. Rillieux patented a method that eliminated the most perilous part of the sugar refining process, the Jamaica Train. This process required slaves to transfer boiling cane juice through a series of four separately heated kettles. Rillieux's new design allowed for more sugar to be produced at a higher quality, with less manpower, and lower associated costs. The new evaporative process made it possible for the United States to dominate the global sugar market and is still used to freeze-dry many items.

Courtesy of Library of Congress Prints and Photographs Division, Washington, DC.

Paul Cuffee

(1800)

By 1800, Paul Cuffee amassed a fortune of nearly $10,000 from investments in ships and waterfront property which included a farm and windmill. At the time of his death, his estate was estimated at $20,000. He was reputed to be the wealthiest person of African descent in the U.S. prior to the War of 1812. Cuffee was also an advocate of the "Back to Africa" movement; in 1815, he, along with 38 African-American emigrants, traveled to Sierra Leone not only for a new life, but also to establish trade between the United States and Africa that did not involve slaves.

National Negro Convention

(1855)

In 1855, an assessment of the net worth of African-American business by region was presented at the National Negro Convention. Midwestern states, which included Ohio, Illinois, and Michigan, represented $1.5 million. Massachusetts, Maine, and Rhode Island, representing New England, had businesses valued at $2 million. New York and Pennsylvania had businesses worth $3 million. These figures are particularly significant given that they have not been adjusted for inflation. The National Negro Convention was an annual meeting of African-American leaders, mostly northern business owners, in which they discussed ways of improving economic opportunities for Blacks. The 1855 convention was the final meeting before the Civil War.

Carla Ann Harris

(1962)

Carla Ann Harris was born in 1962. Harris's work has been celebrated in many of the leading mainstream and African-American business magazines. She has been recognized by *Essence* as one of "50 Women Who are Shaping the World," by *Black Enterprise* as one of the "Top 50 African-Americans on Wall Street" and by *Forbes* as one of the "50 Most Powerful Black Executives in Corporate America." Harris began working as an investment banker for Morgan Stanley in 1985. She has since risen to the position of Managing Director in Global Capital Markets for the financial powerhouse. Presently, she is serving as the Chair of the Private Placement Commitment Equity Committee and a senior member of the Equity Syndicate desk.

Elaine B. Jenkins

(1970)

After working for twenty years as a teacher in the Denver Public School System where she was one of the first African-American teachers, Elaine B. Jenkins changed careers in 1970 and founded One America, Inc. in Washington, DC. One America offered affirmative action planning, rehabilitation counseling, program design and data processing. Jenkins was passionate about seeing to it that more Black women become business leaders. Jenkins worked to help Black businesswomen develop and strengthen their business plans. The family run business became an international business consulting firm by 1973. One America, Inc. was named one of the top 100 Black-owned businesses in America.

Dudley Products

(1967)

In 1967, a husband and wife team from Brooklyn, New York launched a company that continues to become a leader in the African-American hair care products industry. Joe L. Dudley and his wife Eunice founded Dudley Products in the kitchen of their Greensboro, North Carolina home. After more than four decades of continued expansion, Dudley Products manufactures and distributes more than 400 professional and retail ethnic hair products and cosmetics. Through a direct marketing campaign that targets cosmetologists as well as hair and beauty professionals in the United States, the company has earned the label "Avon of the Ethnic Salon Business."

Theodore Martin Alexander

(1931)

In 1931, Theodore Martin Alexander founded Alexander & Company which became one of the oldest and most successful Black firms in Atlanta, GA. During the Montgomery bus boycott in 1956, White-owned insurance companies cancelled the liability insurance policies on the vehicles used by boycotters. Dr. Martin Luther King, Jr. reached out to Alexander who contacted Lloyd's of London Insurance Company to obtain new coverage.

The Freedmen's Bureau Bill

(1865)

The Freedmen's Bureau Bill which created the Freedmen's Bureau was passed by Congress on March 3, 1865. The Bureau provided assistance to former slaves in the form of education, health care, and employment. It also became an important part of Reconstruction by allocating funds to distribute food and help freedmen construct new housing, establish 4,000 schools, and build over 100 hospitals.

Photographs and Prints Division, Schomburg Center for Research in Black Culture, The New York Public Library, Astor, Lenox and Tildan Foundation.

Elijah McCoy

(1872)

In 1872, Elijah McCoy obtained his first patent for his lubrication cup. He worked as a locomotive fireman for the Michigan Central Railroad. He was responsible for manually applying oil and coal to the engines. After doing this for two years, McCoy invented a lubricating cup to create a continual flow of oil over the gears. This cup became such an integral part of the industry that it became known as "the real McCoy." In 1920, McCoy joined with investors and founded the Elijah McCoy Manufacturing Company in Detroit.

Lottie H. Watkins

(1960)

During the 1960's, Lottie H. Watkins became the first African-American real estate broker in Atlanta, Georgia. Watkins was also CEO and founder of her own real estate agency, Lottie Watkins Enterprises, Inc., which specializes in property management. Watkins is the winner of many awards such as the Pioneer in Real Estate Award, the Outstanding Achievement in Real Estate and Business Award and the Atlanta Business League Trail Blazer Award.

William Bonaparte, Jr.

(1963)

In 1963, William Bonaparte, Jr. became the first Private Business Exchange (PBX) installer for Illinois Bell. Born in 1942, Bonaparte later founded his own wiring company, Bonaparte Connections, in 1986, after the Bell Telephone System ceased operations. By 1990, Bonaparte Connections had revenues up to $2 million. In 1991, he formed an electrical contracting firm, the Bonaparte Corporation. Both ventures proved to be quite lucrative, with more than $8.5 million in revenue in 1996. Bonaparte also founded Bonaparte Properties, a restoration contracting firm, in 1999.

Capital Savings Bank of Washington

(1888)

In 1888, Capital Savings Bank was the first Black bank in Washington, DC. Capital Savings Bank was instrumental in the growth of many African-American--owned businesses by providing the capital essential to the growth of black businesses. African-American churches and fraternal organizations played a major role in the development of Capital Savings Bank.

Ronald D. McNeil

(1952)

Allstate Insurance Company's Neighborhood Partnership Plan, their main urban growth initiative, is the work of insurance industry pioneer Ronald D. McNeil. Born in Detroit Michigan in 1952, McNeil was the first and only African-American Finance Officer for the company. In a career that spanned more than three decades, McNeil was elected to four Senior Management Team positions, served as Chairman for two of Allstate's subsidiaries, and acted as President of three local Allstate companies. McNeil, then Senior Vice President of Protection Distribution with more than 70,000 employees working under him, retired in 2007. He had fiscal and leadership responsibilities totaling $30 billion.

Barney L. Ford

(1860)

Escaped slave Barney L. Ford followed the Gold Rush to Colorado in 1860. Because he was African-American, Ford was denied the right to stake a claim in his own name. He was advised by a friendly lawyer to put the deed in the lawyer's name while keeping the gold profits. Ford was cheated out of his claim when the "friendly" lawyer had him legally thrown off the mountain. Though unsuccessful as a gold miner, Ford thrived as the owner of a barber shop and the People's Restaurant. He opened the Inter-Ocean Hotel in 1874. He is remembered as the first African-American businessman in Breckenridge, Colorado.

| 15 |

Lilla St. John

(1953)

It wasn't until 1953 that the New York Stock Exchange (NYSE) exam was passed by the first African-American woman, Lilla St. John, who gave up her former career as a singer and television host because she found this new venture "utterly fascinating." Because of this feat, St. John was able to work as a certified investment counselor for Oppenheimer & Co., one of the nation's oldest investment firms.

Courtesy of ALelia Bundles Bundles.

Madame C.J. Walker

(1867) Madame C.J. Walker was born Sarah Breedlove December 23, 1867. Walker was born to former slaves on a plantation in Louisiana. Without formal schooling, the former laundress and farm laborer became one of the foremost African-American businesswomen of her time. Walker founded her own company, creating hair products, toiletries, and cosmetics for African-American women. For over a year, Walker traveled throughout the Southeast and South, selling her products door to door. In 1908, Walker relocated to Pittsburgh and founded Lelia College, a place where Walker "hair culturists" could be trained. Walker would eventually become one of the first female African-American millionaires.

Arthur Winston

(1906) Arthur Winston born March 22, 1906, holds the record for being the most reliable worker ever chronicled by the United States Department of Labor. He holds the distinction of working for the Los Angeles Metro system for 72 years. At age 10, Winston began working in the cotton fields. After high school, he went to work for the Pacific Electric Railway Company.

Velda Jones-Potter

Velda Jones-Potter was an Executive Vice President at MBNA America Bank–now Bank of America–and started her own consulting firm, Jones-Potter and Associates. Appointed State Treasurer of Delaware, Jones-Potter was sworn into the position to replace the then Governor-elect Jack Markell. In 2009, she became **(2009)** Delaware's first African-American State Treasurer. As Delaware's Treasurer, Mrs. Jones-Potter serves as co-chairperson of the State of Delaware Deferred Compensation Council. She also serves on the Strategic Economic Development Council, the Delaware Board of Pardons, the Delaware Economic and Financial Advisory Council (DEFAC), the Delaware Agricultural Lands Preservation Foundation, the State Employees Benefit Committee (SEBC), and the Delaware Cash Management Policy Board.

Dempsey J. Travis

(1953)

During the 1950's, it was exceedingly difficult for even the wealthiest of African-Americans to be approved for mortgages. In 1953, Dempsey J. Travis established the Sivart Mortgage Company in Chicago, Illinois. Sivart secured financial backing for mortgages, allowing African-Americans to relocate into Chicago's Douglas Park neighborhood. Passionate about building a housing market for minorities, Travis served as president over the Dearborn Real Estate Board. In 1959, he served as the first vice president of the National Association of Real Estate Brokers, a Black organization advocating democracy in housing. Travis also organized the United Mortgage Bankers of America, a mortgage banking association for Blacks.

Stacy Davis

(1999)

Stacy Davis became the first African-American president and CEO of the Fannie Mae Foundation on September 16, 1999. Davis also served as Vice President for Housing and Community Development for Fannie Mae's Southeastern Regional Office in Atlanta where she directed efforts to develop innovative housing partnerships to address the needs of low and moderate income residents.

Charles F. Harris

(1960)

In 1960, the first series of books that offered minority histories for both the educational market and lay readers was launched. The Zenith Book Series was created by Charles F. Harris who was working as an editor for Doubleday Publishing Company at the time. Harris went on to create and manage Howard University Press in 1971 and found Amistad Press Inc. in 1986. Amistad specialized in publishing works by and about African-Americans. Harris sold Amistad in 1999 to HarperCollins Publishing. Today, Harris is running Alpha Zenith Media Inc., another publishing company he founded in 2003.

| 17 |

(1946) ### Theophile T. Allain

Theophile T. Allain, born October 1, 1946, was a farmer, merchant, politician and entrepreneur from Baton Rouge Parish, Louisiana. Allain brokered deals with leading southern commercial businessmen which resulted in creating his own personal wealth. He employed over 30 people, had investments which included land for sugar crops, rice, cattle, and a grocery store. Allain also purchased a plantation for his family.

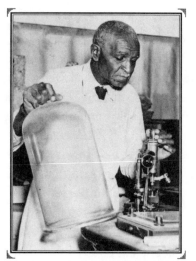

Photographs and Prints Division, Schomburg Center for Research in Black Culture, The New York Public Library, Astor, Lenox and Tildan Foundation.

George Washington Carver

(1864)

Born in 1864, George Washington Carver invented hundreds of commercial uses for the peanut. His research paved the way for sharecroppers to generate additional means of revenue. He shared this research through instructional bulletins. Ultimately, Carver's research helped to revitalize the agricultural landscape of the South. In 1896, Carver was invited to lead the Agriculture Department at the five-year-old Tuskegee Normal and Industrial Institute, later Tuskegee University. Carver accepted the position and remained there for 47 years, teaching former slaves and their descendants farming techniques for self-sufficiency.

The Equal Pay Act of 1963

(1963)

The Equal Pay Act of 1963 requires that men and women be given equal pay for equal work in the same establishment. The jobs need not be identical, but they must be substantially similar. In 2009, this Act was expanded into the Fair Pay Act, which includes prohibitions on pay based upon race, sex and national origin. Both the Equal Pay Act and the Fair Pay Act were amendments to the Fair Labor Standards Act (FLSA) of 1938, which set a national minimum wage, promised a "time and a half" rate for overtime, and ended child labor.

Norma Merrick Sklarek

(1950)

In 1950, not only was Norma Merrick Sklarek the first African-American woman to be licensed as an architect in the nation, she was also the first African-American woman to establish her own architectural firm. Siegel, Sklarek, Diamond was the largest architectural firm owned and operated by women. Sklarek's designs include the U.S. Embassy in Tokyo and such California structures as City Hall in San Bernardino, the Fox Plaza in San Francisco, and Terminal One at Los Angeles International Airport.

E.T. Williams

(1969)

In 1969, E.T. Williams, the founder of Elnora, Inc., a privately-owned family investment company, became the first African American commercial bank officer in the state of Maryland. Williams was also Chairman of the Board and Head of the Fordham Hill Project, the largest eviction co-op conversion in the history of New York City.

Harold E. Doley, Jr.

(1973)

With the help of two New Orleans banks, Harold E. Doley, Jr. became the first and only African-American to buy his own seat on the NYSE in 1973, paying $90,000 for the seat and using his own property – a two-story family house – as collateral. Doley also founded Doley Securities, LLF, the oldest Black-owned investment banking firm in the United States. An initial supporter for Jesse Jackson's Wall Street Project, Doley also served as the U.S. ambassador to the African Development Bank, which was a finance institution owned by fifty African and twenty-five non-African countries from 1983-1985.

Naomi Sims

(1973)

In 1973, Naomi Sims, the first African-American supermodel, created the Naomi Sims Collection. This wig line successfully mimicked the texture of African-American hair. Sales exceeded $5,000,000 in its first year. Sims promptly expanded the company internationally. In 1986, she founded a cosmetics line called Naomi Sims Beauty Products.

| 19 |

Anthony Crawford

(1865)

Anthony Crawford was born a slave in 1865, in Abbeville, South Carolina. During the Reconstruction he was permitted to go to school, though his attendance required that he walk seven miles each way. Crawford went on to work for his former owner, and later made a name for himself as a farmer and community leader. He owned over 400 acres of land in the late 1800s and was believed to have "the prettiest cotton land in the country." Arguably the most affluent African-American in the Abbeville area, Crawford's net worth was estimated at $ 20,000 in the early 1900s.

Courtesy of Library of Congress Prints and Photographs Division, Washington, DC.

Pickney Benton Stewart Pinchback

(1872)

Pinckney Benton Stewart (P.B.S.) Pinchback is best known as the first and only African-American governor to serve during the Reconstruction era. However, Pinchback was also a formidable entrepreneur. In 1870, he became joint owner of the New Orleans Louisianan, a newspaper that was published as both the *Semi-Weekly Louisianan* and the *Weekly Louisianan*. In 1872, Pinchback's partners withdrew from the venture, leaving Pinchback as the sole publisher in control of all stocks. Pinchback also served as the chairman of the Convention of Colored Newspaper Men in 1875 and influenced the formation of the Associated Negro Press (ANP).

Jolyn Robichaux

(1967)

In 1967, Jolyn Robichaux and her husband bought the Baldwin Ice Cream Company, the first Black-owned ice cream company in Chicago. When her husband died in 1971, Robichaux became President and CEO of the company. Under her leadership, the Baldwin Ice Cream Company's sales topped $5 million by 1985. That same year, Jolyn Robichaux became the first African-American woman to be named National Minority Entrepreneur of the Year.

Broadway Federal Bank

(1946)

Broadway Federal Bank opened its doors in 1946. An African-American--owned financial institution in Los Angeles, California, Broadway was founded to meet the economic needs of the city's African-American residents after World War II. The mutual savings and loan institution opened with a capitalization of only $150,000. Broadway has maintained its commitment to hire, train, and mentor community residents. Additionally, the bank donates funds and meeting space to community and religious organizations, and contracts for services with community businesses.

Sarah Gammon Bickford

(1855)

Sarah Gammon Bickford was the only African-American woman in Montana to own a utility company. Born in 1855, Bickford was a former slave who became a businesswoman. She and her husband acquired a part of the water system that supplied drinking water to the town of Virginia City, Montana. Bickford assumed ownership of the water company and supervised all business aspects of the company. Following the death of her husband in 1900, Bickford expanded her holdings, and acquired natural springs. She also built a reservoir to meet the growing demands of the region's population.

Paul R. Williams

(1953)

Known as the "Architect of the Stars," Paul R. Williams won the NAACP's Spingarn Medal for his architectural works in 1953, and was also recognized as the first African-American member of the American Institute of Architects. Earning his moniker throughout his career, Williams built homes for celebrities such as Frank Sinatra, Cary Grant and Lucille Ball. In addition, Williams designed the Saks Fifth Avenue department store in Beverly Hills, California and executed changes for the landmark Beverly Wilshire Hotel.

Newport Gardner

(1780)

In 1780, Newport Gardner founded the African Union Society. It was the first Black mutual aid society in the United States. The mission of Gardner's organization was to assist African-Americans, especially in times of social, political, and economic stress. The society provided benefits for children and widows, as well as apprenticeships to local youth, and loans for those who needed them. The African Union Society created a school for Black children and a night school for the adults in order to help them to elevate themselves in American society.

| 21 |

Marianne Spraggins

(1990)

In 1990, Marianne Spraggins became the first African-American female managing director on Wall Street while working at Smith Barney Shearson. Today, Spraggins is the President of Buy Hold America, a consulting company dedicated to introducing AIC, Ltd. – known as Canada's largest privately-owned mutual fund money management company – to the American market.

Courtesy of Library of Congress Prints and Photographs Division, Washington, DC.

A. Philip Randolph

(1889)

A. Philip Randolph, who was born April 15, 1889, founded the all-Black Brotherhood of Sleeping Car Porters in 1925. This organization of poorly paid men and women who worked on railroad sleeping cars became the first major African-American trade union, and the first chartered by the American Federation of Labor (AFL). He served as the Brotherhood's first president. Randolph also became the first African-American to serve as the International Vice President of the AFL-CIO. In 1965, the A. Philip Randolph Institute was formed to promote the ideas of trade unionism and civil rights for African-Americans, and Randolph served as its first president.

Reverend Leon H. Sullivan

(1964)

As a child, Reverend Leon H. Sullivan supported himself by collecting and reselling discarded bottles. In 1964, Reverend Sullivan founded Opportunities Industrialization Center of America, Inc. to provide job training for Blacks hoping to enter the job market. He also led boycotts of businesses to force the hiring of minority workers. Reverend Sullivan served on the board of General Motors, making him the first African-American to serve on the board of a major U.S. corporation.

Robert Reed Church, Sr.

(1874)

In 1874, Robert Reed Church, Sr. founded the Solvent Savings Bank and Trust Company in Memphis, TN to encourage African-Americans to manage and save their earnings. In 1908, when the Beale Street Baptist Church (today's First Baptist Church of Beale Street) was facing foreclosure by creditors, Robert R. Church and the bank came to Beale Street Baptist Church's rescue and paid off its creditors with liberal repayment terms. Church also constructed a multi-purpose facility, valued at $100,000 when built, Church's Park and Auditorium, for Blacks in the community. He was the South's first African-American millionaire.

The Pace Phonographic Corporation

(1921)

In 1921, The Pace Phonographic Corporation, which issued records on the Black Swan Label, was the first record company owned and operated by an African-American, Harry Pace. By the summer of 1922, the company which had begun in Pace's basement now had a staff of 30 employees including its own 8- man orchestra, 7 district managers in the major cities, and over 1,000 dealers and agents in locations as diverse as the Philippines and the West Indies. After Black Swan declared bankruptcy in December 1923, Pace moved on to open the Northeastern Life Insurance Company which became one of the largest Black owned businesses in the North.

Glegg Watson

(1982)

Black Life in Corporate America: Swimming in the Mainstream was published in August of 1982 by Glegg Watson. The book highlights research on gender and racial experiences in Fortune 500 companies that Waston collected for his unfinished dissertation. With George Davis, Watson interviewed more than 160 African-American managers, their superiors, and others. They found that American corporations at the time reflected the same feelings that encourage discrimination in the workplace. The book later became a national bestseller and established Watson and Davis as experts on the subject of race and business.

Clara McLaughlin

(1984)

When she purchased KLMG (later renamed KFXK) in Longview, Texas in 1984, Clara McLaughlin became the first African-American woman to own a television station. She later acquired three other television stations in Texas. McLaughlin intended the stations to be part of the East Texas Television Network, of which she was the chairman and CEO. In 2002, McLaughlin bought *The Florida Star,* which is the largest, oldest, and most widely read Black-owned newspaper in northeast Florida and southern Georgia. She presently serves as editor of *The Florida Star.*

| 23 |

Ruth Jean Bowen

(1959)

Ruth Jean Bowen founded Queens Booking Corporation in 1959, at one time the largest Black-owned talent agency in the world. Its mission was to create opportunities for Black performers. Bowen worked with entertainers such as Dinah Washington, Aretha Franklin, Ray Charles, Sammy Davis, Jr., and her first husband, William (Billy) Bowen, one of the original Ink Spots.

Provident Hospital and Training School for Nurses, Chicago.

The first hospital and school established in this country by colored people for their own race. The founder, Dr. D. H. Williams is one of the best surgeons in the country. 100 graduates have gone out from the school.

Photographs and Prints Division, Schomburg Center for Research in Black Culture, The New York Public Library, Astor, Lenox and Tildan Foundation.

Provident Hospital

(1891) Provident Hospital in Chicago, founded by Dr. Daniel Hale Williams in 1891, was the first African-American-owned and operated hospital in the United States. It was a teaching hospital where African-American doctors and nurses were trained. While the founders' initial priority was to secure an adequate hospital building, they also considered community needs, the initial scope of services, and the Hospital's overall mission. The Hospital's first annual budget totaled $5,429. The first physician in surgical training, Dr. Austin Curtis, received two years of instruction under Dr. Williams. (Dr. Curtis later became the first Black surgeon-in-chief at Freedmen's Hospital in Washington, DC.)

(1980) Ursula Burns

Ursula Burns began as an intern at Xerox in 1980 and worked her way up, eventually becoming the senior vice president of Corporate Strategic Services and later president in 2007. Burns became the first African-American woman to head a Fortune 500 company when she became the CEO of the Xerox Corporation in 2009.

Bertram M. Lee and Peter C.B. Bynoe

(1989) In 1989, the Denver Nuggets of the National Basketball Association (NBA) became the first Black-owned, major professional sports franchise when they were purchased by Boston investor Bertram M. Lee and Illinois sports facilities manager Peter C.B. Bynoe for a reported $65 million.

Kenneth I. Chenault

(2001)

In 2001, Kenneth I. Chenault was named President and Chief Operating Officer of American Express. He is the third African-American to become a CEO of a Fortune 500 company. Under his leadership, American Express experienced significant financial growth through innovative approaches and branding. Increasing the company's market share, Chenault led AMEX's campaign to build links with banks, changing the company's traditional policy of only issuing cards directly to consumers. One of Chenault's proudest accomplishments was signing Tiger Woods to an AMEX contract. A native of Long Island, NY, Chenault graduated from Bowdoin College and Harvard University Law School.

Emanuel Manna and Mary Baroon

(1736)

Emanuel Manna and his wife Mary Baroon launched a catering enterprise and an oyster and ale house in Providence, Rhode Island in 1736. The husband and wife business team were former slaves who had purchased their own freedom. Their businesses were started at a time when free African-Americans had few avenues for pursing economic independence. Catering was a particularly lucrative option for budding African-American entrepreneurs in the North at the time.

Sarah Spencer Washington

(1920)

In 1920, Sarah Spencer Washington established the Apex News and Hair Company in Atlantic City, New Jersey. In addition to a chain of beauty schools that spanned the nation and the globe, the company owned the Apex Drug Store. In 1939, Washington was honored as one of the "Most Distinguished Business women" at the New York World's Fair.

| 25 |

Earvin "Magic" Johnson, Jr.

(1987)

Earvin "Magic" Johnson, Jr. was a successful basketball player from the late 1970s to the mid 1990s. In 1987, Johnson formed Magic Johnson Enterprises. Serving as Chairman and CEO, Johnson expanded the company and its subsidiaries to include a chain of movie theaters, a promotional company, a movie studio and a joint venture with Starbucks. Its net worth is $700 million. Johnson also serves as Vice-President of the Lakers (his former team) and is a minority owner of the team.

Courtesy of the Afro-American Newspapers Archives and Research Center.

AFRO American Newspapers

(1892) John Henry Murphy, Sr. was born into slavery in 1840 in Baltimore, Maryland. Freed by the Emancipation Proclamation, Murphy went on to establish a newspaper for the local church community in 1892. *The Baltimore Afro-American* began with the merger of Murphy's own church newspaper, *The Sunday School Helper,* with *The Ledger,* another church publication, and an earlier version of the *Afro-American* which had been founded by Reverend William M. Alexander. Murphy purchased the original paper and printing equipment for $200. Under Murphy's direction, the *Baltimore Afro-American* became one of the most prominent African-American newspapers of the 20th century.

Eta Phi Beta

(1943) In 1943, Eta Phi Beta was incorporated in Detroit, Michigan. The sorority for African-American businesswomen was established to provide vital connections for African-American business and professional women. These connections allowed women to share their unique talents with each other and the greater community. The founders were Ann Porter, Earlene Carter, Katherine R. Douglas, Atheline Shelton Graham, Mattie Rankin, Ethel Madison, Merry Green Hubbard, Mae Edwards Curry, Ivy Burt Banks, Dorothy Sylvers Brown, and Lena Reed. All of the founders were students of Lewis Business College.

Second Morrill Act

(1890) Proceeds of governmental land grants began to include Black institutions with the passing of the Second Morrill Act in 1890. Under the Morrill Act, the Federal Government committed to grant each state 30,000 acres of public land issued in the form of "land scrip" certificates for each of its Representatives and Senators in Congress. The proceeds of this land were to be used to fund public colleges that focused on agriculture and mechanic arts. In 1862, President Abraham Lincoln signed into law what was then known as 'An Act Donating Public Lands to the Mechanic Arts.'

Target Market News, Inc.

(1988)

Target Market News, Inc. is considered one of the leading authorities on marketing, advertising, and media directed to the African-American market. Since 1988, the company's trade publication, *Target Market News*, has covered news and information related to the Black consumer market. Its annual report, "The Buying Power of Black America," analyzes how African-American consumers spend billions of dollars in hundreds of product and service categories.

Bella Marshall Barden

(1982)

At age 32, Bella Marshall Barden became one of the youngest African-American women to head the financial department of a major American city. In 1982, Barden was named Finance Director for the city of Detroit, Michigan. When she assumed responsibility for the fiscal health of Detroit, the city was in dire economic straits. In just over a decade, Barden had Detroit well on its way to a strong recovery. *Essence* magazine lauded Barden as one of the richest African-American women in the country, with an estimated net worth of $25 million.

Marcus Books

(1960)

Julian and Raye Richardson co-founded one of the nation's oldest African-American bookstores, Success Bookstore, which was later renamed Marcus Books to honor Marcus Garvey. Founded in 1960 Marcus Books was a meeting place for activist groups, and one of the first business establishments in San Francisco to host regular book clubs and poetry slams. A second location was opened in Oakland in the mid 1970s, and the San Francisco store settled into its current location on Fillmore in 1980.

Mannie Jackson

(1993)

As owner and president of the Harlem Globetrotters, Mannie Jackson was the first African-American owner of a major international sports organization. Jackson bought the beleaguered Globetrotters for $6 million in 1993. The organization had been failing due to aging stars and old, repetitious routines. After assuming control, Jackson let go of the old stars, replaced them with new talent, and updated the music and routines. His changes paid off: the Harlem Globetrotters became a successful, family-friendly alternative to the NBA.

Photographs and Prints Division, Schomburg Center for Research in Black Culture, The New York Public Library, Astor, Lenox and Tildan Foundation.

Atlanta Compromise

(1895)

During the Cotton States and International Exposition in Atlanta, GA in 1895, Booker T. Washington delivered his "Atlanta Compromise" speech in response to the "Negro Problem," or what to do about the abysmal socio-economic conditions of Blacks and the relationship between the races in the economically shifting, post-Reconstruction South. This "Compromise" called upon Whites to take the responsibility for improving social and economic relations between the races. He asked Whites to trust Blacks and provide them with more opportunities so that both races could advance in industry and agriculture.

Dorothy Brunson

(1969)

In 1969, Dorothy Brunson co-founded Howard Sanders Advertising, one of the first Black advertising agencies in America. Brunson left with $115,000 in buy-out money the following year. Brunson was tapped by Inner City Broadcasting to organize investors for its radio stations. Brunson was key in Inner City's expansion from a company with $500,000 in annual sales to one that owned seven major-market radio stations, exceeding $23 million. Most notably, Brunson is the first African-American to own a full-power radio station, WGTW-TV. She eventually purchased three other radio stations, expanding her market to New Jersey, Delaware, and Pennsylvania.

Barbara Bowles

(1989)

In 1989, Barbara Bowles became Chicago's first African-American female equity manager when she founded the Kenwood Group. Bowles has managed many high-profile clients including Quaker Oats, Abbott Laboratories, and the Chicago Transit Authority. She also launched a mutual fund with the debut of the Kenwood Growth and Income Fund, making her the first African-American to do so.

Orion Publishing Company

(1901)

Orion Publishing Company was one of the first African-American commercial trade book publishing firms in the United States. It was established in 1901, by Reverend Sutton E. Griggs. Grigg's intention was to sell books to the growing African-American market. The works published by Orion were predominantly novels which combined facts and fiction to present the plight of an oppressed people as well as solutions. These novels focused on the political issues, the image, and the dignity and survival of Black Americans.

Hobart T. Taylor, Sr.

(1932)

In 1932, Hobart T. Taylor, Sr. purchased a taxi cab franchise in Houston, Texas. Governed by the segregation laws of the day, African-American customers were only permitted to ride in cabs operated by African-American drivers. The high number of unpaved roads in African-American communities rapidly decreased the lifespan of many cabs. Attempting to find a solution to the problem, Taylor designed a car engine that would extend the lifespan of a cab from two to five years. Taylor was a millionaire by 1940, and his business was valued at $5 million by 1970.

People's Grocery Company

(1800s)

In the late 1800's, People's Grocery Company was founded in Memphis, Tennessee by three black men: Thomas Moss, Calvin McDowell, and Henry Stewart. From the day it opened, this business became the target of White resentment. In 1892, the owners were lynched by an angry White mob, prompting Ida B. Wells to publish Southern Horrors: Lynch Law in All Its Phases.

| 29 |

Joseph Lee

(1849)

Joseph Lee, who was born in 1849, was a man of many accomplishments. For instance, Lee was the owner and manager of the Woodland Park Hotel in Newton, Massachusetts. Lee also opened a catering business in 1902 called the Lee Catering Company. He also operated a resort specializing in seafood called the Squantum Inn. In June of 1895, Lee patented a device that mechanized tearing, crumbling and grinding bread into crumbs. The idea came to him while trying to find other uses for day-old bread. The crumbling machine became a major restaurant tool. Lee later sold his patent.

Courtesy of Library of Congress Prints and Photographs Division, Washington, DC.

National Association of Colored Women's Club

(1896) The National Association of Colored Women's Clubs (NACWC) was founded in 1896 to work for the moral, economic, social, and religious welfare of women and children. The NACWC grew out of the merger of two nationally representative organizations, the Colored Women's League of Washington and the National Federation of Afro-American Women. Mary Church Terrell was elected the organization's first president in 1896 and served until 1900. Currently known as the National Association of Colored Women, this organization is now the oldest African-American secular group working for the defense and well-being of women and youth.

Herman Jerome Russell

(1959) In 1959, Herman Jerome Russell founded the H.J. Russell Construction Company. While the company initially focused on the construction of duplexes and single family homes, they soon expanded and began taking on other projects. Perhaps the most well-known of these projects was a joint-venture with C.P. Moody Construction, another African-American owned company. Together, the two firms built the Olympic Stadium in Atlanta for the 1996 Summer Olympics, officially known as the Games of the XXVI Olympiad. Today, Russell serves as the Chairman of the company, whose name is now H.J. Russell & Company. Herman J. Russell served as the first African-American member of the Atlanta Chamber of Commerce. Russell was later the Chamber's first African-American president.

Marjorie Stewart Joyner

(1916) The "Grand Dame of Black Beauty Culture," Marjorie Stewart Joyner was a pioneering inventor and educator in African-American beauty culture. In 1916, Joyner opened her own shop and soon met Madame C.J. Walker at a training course. This began a partnership that found Joyner the director of Walker's national chain of beauty schools. In 1926, she became the first African-American woman to receive a patent for an invention. Her patented permanent wave machine allowed women to maintain their hairstyles for several days after they left the beautician's chair. Joyner was also a major fundraiser for African- American colleges, including Bethune-Cookman.

Samuel B. Fuller

(1947)

With a $25 investment, Samuel B. Fuller founded Fuller Products Company, a door-to-door cosmetic company. Determined to expand his business, in 1947, Fuller acquired Boyer International Laboratories. Fuller's customers were primarily in the South: Atlanta, Birmingham, Montgomery, Dallas, and several locales in North Carolina. Business soared after the acquisition of Boyer and by the early 1960s sales peaked at $10 million. Fuller had a line of 300 products and employed 5,000 salespeople.

M. Carl Holman

(1968)

Carl Holman became Vice President of Programs at the National Urban Coalition, an organization that formed after the 1967 summer riots, in 1968. He later became president of the organization in 1971, earning the honor of being the first African-American to head the National Urban Coalition. He advocated for programs in housing, education, employment, job training and economic development.

Mechanics and Farmers (M&F) Bank

(1909)

The Mechanics and Farmers (M&F) Bank opened in Durham, North Carolina on August 1, 1909. In 1935, it became the first lending institution in North Carolina to receive a Certificate of Authority from the Federal Housing Administration. The bank stimulated Black entrepreneurship in the state. The name reflects two sides of North Carolina's economy. "Mechanics," from the legal phrase "mechanics lien" refers to the fact that many business leaders from different occupations helped found, and benefit from M&F Bank. "Farmers" refers to how ownership of real property, specifically farmland, influenced the state's economy.

Colored Farmers' Alliance

(1886)

In 1886, African-American farmers in the South joined forces to create the Colored Farmers' Alliance. Their aim was to compel the federal, state, and local governments to help struggling African-American farmers. To do this, the Alliance published a newspaper, the National Alliance, established exchanges throughout the South to sell goods and obtain loans, raised funds to extend public school terms and sometimes funded schools. By 1892, the Alliance had more than 1.2 million active members.

Courtesy of Library of Congress Prints and Photographs Division, Washington, DC.

National Negro Business League

(1900) The National Negro Business League was founded by Booker T. Washington in 1900 to promote commercial, agricultural, educational, and industrial advancement as well as the financial development of Black people. Washington was hoping that the League would encourage Blacks to start their own businesses, gain the right to vote, and seek due process under the law. The League's membership included a number of successful Black business owners and professionals as well as a large number of middle class Blacks who were looking to start their own businesses. The League operated through state and local chapters, many of which were located in the South. League meetings were held to allow small business owners to network with each other and share stories of their struggles and successes.

Tony Brown

(1980) Television executive, producer, columnist, educator, filmmaker, and activist Tony Brown founded Black College Day in 1980. Brown was the first and founding dean of the School of Communications at Howard University. He formed the Council for Economic Development of Black Americans in 1985. Buy Freedom was its best known campaign. African-American consumers patronized Black-owned businesses that displayed the freedom seal. The freedom seals were only distributed to businesses that pledged courtesy, competitive prices, employment opportunities, discounts, and active community involvement.

Sean Combs

(1993) Leaving an internship at Uptown Records, Sean Combs founded Bad Boy Records in 1993. Although known primarily as a hip-hop artist and producer, Combs has also enjoyed great success venturing in clothing (the Sean John line), films, restaurants, and men's fragrances. Combs was named one of *Fortune* magazine's 40 Richest People Under 40 in 2002 and, by 2006, could claim a net worth of $346 million.

Ophelia DeVore

(1946)

In 1946, Ophelia DeVore and a few friends established the Grace Del Marco Agency, one of the first modeling agencies in America to focus on the ethnic market. The modeling agency paved the way for African-Americans in the industry. DeVore also hosted ABC's Spotlight on Harlem as an opportunity to increase her agency's exposure. In 1985, her enterprise went global, with Swaziland as a client. DeVore also owns The Columbus Times, a newspaper founded by her late husband. She also served as a consultant to many Fortune 500 companies.

Edwin C. Berry

(1854)

Edwin C. Berry was born in Oberlin, Ohio in 1854. In 1892, Berry purchased a piece of property where he built the Hotel Berry. The establishment had fifty-five rooms and boasted an elevator and walk-in closets. The Hotel Berry was one of the most upscale hotels in Athens, Ohio. Berry was also the first hotelier to place bibles in each guest room. Booker T. Washington pronounced Berry to be "the leading hotel-keeper of color" in the country in his book *The Negro Business*. Berry was also an active member of the National Negro Business League.

H.R. George

(1920s)

One of the most recognizable African-American speculators on Wall Street in the 1920's, H.R. George, known as the "Black Wolf of Wall Street," rose to this position by making fearless moves. George earned a fortune on the pre-Depression stock market. His investments and profits were believed to have reached the millions.

| 33 |

Black Manifesto

(1969)

Despite its controversial condemnation of capitalism and its proclamation of a socialist agenda, James Forman's *Black Manifesto* was adopted at the National Black Economic Conference in 1969. The manifesto demanded that White Christian churches and Jewish synagogues pay $500 million in reparations as compensation for past exploitation of the Black community. It also stated that the reparations would be used to fund projects to improve the Black community, including a Southern Land Bank, Black Labor Strike and Defense Fund Training Center, four major enterprises, four television networks, and a Black university.

Photographs and Prints Division, Schomburg Center for Research in Black Culture, The New York Public Library, Astor, Lenox and Tildan Foundation.

Maggie Lena Walker

(1903)

Maggie Lena Walker was the first woman to charter a bank in the United States. In 1903, she founded the St. Luke Penny Savings Bank. Walker was also the first woman to serve as president of a bank, sitting at the helm of St. Luke until 1929. The bank managed to withstand the Great Depression due to Walker's foresight and business savvy. In 1931, she merged the St. Luke Penny Savings Bank with two Richmond, Virginia banks that were also owned by African-Americans.

Caroline Robinson Jones

(1964)

Caroline Robinson Jones became the first African-American woman elected Vice President of a major advertising company, Mingo-Jones, which she co-founded. In 1964, Jones founded her own advertising agency, Caroline Jones, Inc. (formerly Caroline Jones Advertising, Inc.). She also served as Creative Director of J. Walter Thompson Company. She was instrumental in creating the special issue entitled *The J. Walter Thompson Story: Celebrating 100 Years of Advertising.* Jones was known for creating such memorable slogans as L'Oreal's "Because You're Worth It" and Kentucky Fried Chicken's "We Do Chicken Right."

The Freedom's Journal

(1827)

In 1827, *The Freedom's Journal* was the nation's first Black-owned and operated newspaper. Established by free Black men in New York City to counter the racism published in mainstream papers, *The Freedom's Journal* served over 300,000 newly freed Blacks by printing school, job, and housing listings. At various times, the newspaper employed between 14 and 44 agents to collect and renew subscriptions, which cost $3 per year. *Freedom's Journal* was soon circulated in 11 states, the District of Columbia, Haiti, Europe, and Canada. A typical advertisement cost between 25 and 75 cents.

Vince Cullers Advertising

(1956)

Vince Cullers Advertising, established in 1956, was the first African-American-owned, full-service advertising agency and the first to actively target the African-American market. Cullers started out in the late 1940's as a young, eager and skillful talent. Cullers' impressive portfolio landed him job offers, but when he showed up as Black, he suddenly didn't have a job. The Civil Rights Movement helped spark Cullers to start his own company. He employed other African-Americans and inspired them through mentoring. Founder Vincent T. Cullers headed a firm whose clients included the Kellogg Company, Pizza Hut, Sears, Roebuck & Company and the United States Department of Treasury.

William Henry Dean

(1938)

William Henry Dean is an economist who became the Director of the Community Relations Project for the National Urban League. He was also appointed to the Division of Economic Stability and Development for the United Nations where he served as Chief of the Africa Unit. Dean was awarded a Ph.D. in Economics at Harvard in 1938; although he was qualified for a tutorial post, Dean was denied the opportunity because of his race. Ironically, his dissertation, "Theory of Geographical Location of Economic Activity" had been used as an economics text in Harvard and Northwestern Universities.

Garrett A. Morgan

(1923)

In 1923, Garrett A. Morgan patented a technological breakthrough that would change the flow of traffic around the world. Morgan invented one of the first traffic signals in the United States. His technology was later patented in Great Britain and Canada. General Motors purchased Morgan's patent for $ 40,000. Years later, Morgan gained attention for his other invention, the gas mask. On July 25, 1916, Garrett Morgan made national news for using his gas mask to rescue 32 men trapped during an explosion in an underground tunnel 250 feet beneath Lake Erie.

| 35 |

Constructive Alternative Budget Proposal Initiative

(1981)

In 1981, responding to President Reagan's budget for the fiscal year of 1982, the Congressional Black Caucus (CBC) unveiled the Constructive Alternative Budget Proposal Initiative in Washington, DC, becoming the first time the CBC presented a budget for the House floor to debate.

Photographs and Prints Division, Schomburg Center for Research in Black Culture, The New York Public Library, Astor, Lenox and Tildan Foundation.

Mary Mcleod Bethune

(1904)

In 1904, Mary McLeod Bethune founded the Daytona Educational and Industrial Training School for Negro Girls with an initial investment of $1.50. Understandably, as the school at Daytona progressed, it became necessary to secure an adequate financial base. In 1912, Bethune interested James M. Gamble of the Procter & Gamble Company of Cincinnati, Ohio who contributed financially to the school and served as chairman of its board of trustees until his death. In 1923, the school merged with the Cookman Institute for Men, becoming a co-ed high school. It reached university status in 2007 and the institution was renamed Bethune-Cookman University.

Jerry Williams

(1993)

Jerry Williams became the first African-American CEO of a Fortune 500 company when he rose to the position of CEO of AM International, a Chicago-based graphics company. Williams was also the first African-American CEO to grace the cover of *Fortune* magazine. In 1993, Williams founded Grand Eagle Companies in Chicago and served as president and chief executive officer of this $215 million company – the largest independent manufacturer and repairer of electric motors and transformers in North America. In 2000, he sold the company to a private equity group and retired.

Don Coleman

(1988)

Don Coleman, former NFL player and advertising executive, founded one of the nation's largest Black-owned advertising agencies, Don Coleman Associates in 1988. The company exists today as Don Coleman Advertising (DCA). In 1999 DCA joined True North Diversified Companies, under its New America Strategies Group (NASG), the company's multicultural offshoot. True North gained a 49 percent interest in DCA, and named Coleman as the head of NASG. The merger gave DCA the resources of the largest multicultural marketing-firm network in the U.S. and NASG added DCA to its billings, which would increase to about $200 million. NASG also boasted that it was the only partnership with the resources to target the African-American, Hispanic, and Asian markets simultaneously.

W. H. Jefferson Funeral Home

(1894)

Founded in 1894, the W. H. Jefferson Funeral Home is the oldest African-American business in the state of Mississippi. Located in Vicksburg, W. H. Jefferson Funeral Home was founded by William Henry and Lucy Jefferson. Mr. Jefferson was the first African-American funeral director in the state of Mississippi.

Darwin Nathaniel Davis

(1989)

Recognized as one of the 25 most important African-American executives by *Black Enterprise* magazine, Darwin Nathaniel Davis rose from being hired as an Equitable Life Insurance salesman after the 1967 Detroit Riots to become the company's first Black regional president. In 1989, Davis was promoted to senior vice president. A mentor to many young African-American executives, Davis retired as senior vice president of AXA Financial in 1998.

John Forten

(1785)

John Forten was one of the wealthiest African-Americans in post-colonial America. After an apprenticeship under the sail-maker Robert Bridges in 1785, Forten was employed as a foreman. Experimenting with sail types, he invented a revolutionary sail that enabled sailors to achieve greater speeds. Forten purchased a sail loft, employing both Black and White workers. Forten used his substantial wealth to finance the anti-slavery newspaper *The Liberator,* and to build a school for African-American children. He also purchased the freedom of several slaves.

Special Field Order Number 15

(1865)

In 1865, Special Field Order Number 15 called for Georgia Sea Island and thirty miles of land on the Charleston, South Carolina coast to be ceded to newly freed slaves. It was seen as a temporary solution to the problem of newly freed slaves. Special Field Order No. 15 confiscated a strip of coastal land stretching from Charleston to Jacksonville, Florida. The order gave most of the roughly 400,000 acres to newly emancipated slaves in forty-acre sections. Those lands became the basis for the slogan "forty acres and a mule," igniting the belief that ex-slaves throughout the old Confederacy would be given the confiscated lands of former plantation owners.

Courtesy of Library of Congress Prints and Photographs Division, Washington, DC.

W.E.B. DuBois
Niagara Movement

(1905) The Niagara Movement was founded in July 1905 during a three-day meeting of African-American leaders, most notably W.E.B. Du Bois and William Monroe Trotter. Fifty-nine men were invited and 29 attended the first meeting in Fort Erie, Ontario, Canada. The Niagara Movement published the Declaration of Principles which acknowledged the progress made by Negroes and listed several concerns. Foremost among these concerns were suffrage for women, civil liberty, equal economic opportunities, decent housing and neighborhoods, and equal access to education. The Niagara Movement eventually split into separate committees and divided itself among the states, establishing chapters in twenty-one states altogether.

(1993) Grigsby Brandford & Co.

In 1993, Grigsby Brandford & Co., a Black-owned investment bank, beat out Goldman Sachs and Morgan Stanley to lead-manage a $503 million refinancing for the Los Angeles Convention Center. This was the largest municipal bond deal in the city's history at the time.

Bronner Bros. Inc.

(1947) In 1947, brothers Nathaniel H. and Arthur E. Bronner, along with their sister Emma, began their own hair care company. Bronner Bros. Inc. is known for its extensive line of products created for African-American hair, including African Royale. Today, it is one of the largest private African-American hair and skin care producers in the country. The company also sponsors an annual International Beauty and Trade Show, which is the largest show of its kind with thousands of attendees annually from all over the world.

Ernie Green

(1968)

After retiring from the NFL in 1968, Ernie Green co-founded Ernie Green Industries, Inc. (EGI), a manufacturer of automotive parts in Dayton, Ohio. In 1987, Green established Florida Production Engineering (FPE), a wholly-owned subsidiary of (EGI). FPE now ranks among the industry's leading manufacturers of chrome-plated and metal-stamped parts.

(1827) ### Thomas Day

Thomas Day was a wood-wright who worked in Halifax County, Virginia and Caswell County, North Carolina. He built and operated one of North Carolina's largest furniture manufacturing companies. In 1827, Day purchased his shop for $500 in cash. He purchased stock in the State Bank of North Carolina and a Union Tavern. He was also the owner of significant pieces of real estate, including his place of work and residence. Day had twelve employees, both Black and White, working for him and invested more than $ 5,000 in his business.

The Black Community Survival Conference

(1972)

The Black Panthers initiated "Survival Programs" which provided food, clothes, medical services, educational opportunities and community activities for African-Americans and other oppressed people. In 1972, The Black Panthers hosted one of the first "Survival Programs" and called it The Black Community Survival Conference. The Panthers advertised that they would provide 10,000 free bags of groceries.

| 39 |

(1815) ### George DeBaptiste

George DeBaptiste born March 26, 1815 was a free Black who operated a barbershop. He was instrumental in helping slaves escape from Kentucky. Although known as an abolitionist and manager on the Underground Railroad, DeBaptiste was also known as an entrepreneur and businessman. Upon moving to Indiana, the successful abolitionist and businessman challenged a law stating that free Blacks must pay a $150 fee to reside in Indiana. The law was upheld. However, DeBaptiste was rendered exempt.

Courtesy of Library of Congress Prints and Photographs Division, Washington, DC.

Chicago Defender

(1905)

The Chicago Defender was established in 1905 by Robert Sengstacke Abbott. Abbott began the paper with an initial investment of only 25 cents and a press run of 300 copies. By the start of World War I, the *Chicago Defender* was the nation's most influential Black weekly newspaper, with more than two thirds of its readership base located outside of Chicago. Columnists at the *Chicago Defender* included Walter White and Langston Hughes. The paper also published early works by Pulitzer Prize-winning poet Gwendolyn Brooks. Today, the *Chicago Defender* is the flagship publication of Real Times Inc., a media company that also includes among its holdings newspapers in Illinois, Michigan, and Pennsylvania.

The Lincoln Motion Picture Company

(1916)

The Lincoln Motion Picture Company was founded by Black actor Noble Johnson and his brother, George Johnson in 1916 in Omaha, Nebraska. It was incorporated in 1917 in Los Angeles, California for $75,000. Although Lincoln Motion Picture Company only produced five films (two pictorial and three dramatic subjects), it became famous for showcasing Black talent in all facets of cinema. Out of all of their films, the last one, "By Right of Birth" was the only one that accepted White investors.

Eugene Byron Lewis

(1969)

In 1969, Eugene Byron Lewis established the advertising agency, Uniworld Group, Inc. Hitting a recession slump five years later, the company managed to survive because of its million dollars in gross sales stemming from the Black radio soap opera Lewis produced called Sounds of the City. Uniworld is the winner of more than 100 advertising awards today, and continues to handle accounts totaling $157 million.

Sonjia Waller-Young

(1982)

Sonjia Waller-Young founded Eventions, Inc., one of the first minority- and female-owned, full-service communications companies, in 1982. With a client list that includes The Coca-Cola Company, Georgia-Pacific Corporation, and Coors Brewing, Eventions, Inc. is recognized as one of the nation's top event planning/communications companies. Ms. Waller-Young has worked with Maya Angelou, Oprah Winfrey, Harry Belafonte, Muhammad Ali, and other world-renowned celebrities.

James Wormley

(1871)

In 1871, James Wormley, a successful caterer, established the Wormley House. Wormley's Hotel opened its doors. The Washington, DC hotel contained five stories, featured a bar in its basement, a barbershop, and an elegant dining room on the first floor. All guest rooms contained individual telephones. The hotel was founded by successful caterer, James Wormley. Located near the White House at the southwest corner of 15th and H Streets Northwest, Wormley House soon became popular among the wealthy and politically prominent in the nation's capital.

Joseph L. Searles III

(1970)

In 1970, Joseph L. Searles III became the first African-American to serve as a member of the New York Stock Exchange (NYSE). Searles traded securities before selling his seat on the exchange and moving on to corporate finance. In addition, Searles has worked with the Federal Government and numerous state and municipal agencies in the fields of housing, economic development, and urban affairs. As Deputy Commissioner of the New York City Economic Development Administration, Mr. Searles took a leadership role in establishing minority enterprises and small businesses throughout the city by hosting America's first Franchising Fair in 1969.

| 41 |

Bridget "Biddy" Mason

(1818)

Bridget "Biddy" Mason, born August 15, 1818, once an illiterate slave, was one of the first Black women to own land in Los Angeles. Through her real estate and wise business decisions, Mason accumulated nearly $300, 000 in wealth. Mason co-founded and financed the Los Angeles branch of the First African Methodist Episcopal Church, Los Angeles' first Black church in 1872.

Photographs and Prints Division, Schomburg Center for Research in Black Culture, The New York Public Library, Astor, Lenox and Tildan Foundation.

National Urban League

(1920) The mission of the National Urban League, founded in 1920, is to enable African-Americans to secure economic self-reliance, parity, power, and civil rights. The National Urban League grew out of a grassroots movement in reaction to the United States Supreme Court's approval of segregation in the 1896 Plessy v. Ferguson decision. Mrs. Ruth Standish Baldwin and Dr. George Edmund Haynes, who would become the Committee's first executive secretary, were integral to the founding of the organization. The fledgling organization counseled Black migrants from the South, helped train Black social workers, and worked to bring educational and employment opportunities to Blacks. By the end of World War I, the organization had 81 staff members working in 30 cities.

Julian Abele

(1902) In 1902, Julian Abele became the first African-American to graduate from the University of Pennsylvania. An architect, Abele was Chief Designer for the firm of Horace Trumbauer & Associates. Abele was only 27 years old; yet, he was paid a salary of $12, 000 annually, which equates to over $250,000 currently. Abele's design projects included Philadelphia's Free Library and Museum of Art, the James B. Duke mansion in New York, as well as, buildings and chapels for Trinity College, now presently known as Duke University.

McKissack & McKissack

(1905) The oldest African-American architectural firm in the country is McKissack & McKissack. The firm's foundation dates back to Moses McKissack (1790-1865). The firm was founded by Moses McKissack III in 1905. Within a year of opening his Nashville, Tennessee construction company, Moses built a home for the Dean of Architecture and Engineering at Vanderbilt University. He was later commissioned to build the Carnegie Library at Fisk University. Moses subsequently entered into a partnership with his brother Calvin Lunsford McKissack, and the two formed McKissack & McKissack Architects. Moses and Calvin were among the first architects registered by the State of Tennessee in 1912, and in 1922 they incorporated Tennessee's first professional Black design-and-build firm.

Ross Love

(1946)

Ross Love, born May 28, 1946 in Yeadon, PA, was an entrepreneur, philanthropist, and former corporate executive. Love and his business partners bought a radio station that became popular for its talk-show format. He started his own company, Blue Chip Broadcasting, and bought more than 19 Black radio stations in the Midwest. At one point, Love's company was the largest Black-owned radio broadcasting company in the country.

Gabriel Prosser

(1800)

In 1800, Gabriel Prosser was an enslaved blacksmith who planned to lead a slave rebellion in the Richmond area of Virginia. Prosser wanted to combat discrimination against Black slaves-for-hire and business owners. Botched by inclement weather, two slaves leaked information about the rebellion and the governor of Virginia called the state militia to capture Prosser and his co-conspirators. They were successful. Out of those slaves helping Prosser's efforts, 56 slaves were arrested. Slaveholders who lost slaves to execution or banishment were reimbursed for their slaves' value, a total of $8900.

National Domestic Workers Union

(1968)

National Domestic Workers Union, formed in 1968 to improve work conditions and wages, provided training programs, counseling and job placement for domestic workers. It was founded by Dorothy Lee Bolden whom in her earlier career began working as a maid after school, washing diapers for $1.25 per week. At age 12, Bolden began keeping house for $1.50 per week.

| 43 |

Wallace "Wally" Amos, Jr.

(1975)

Wallace "Wally" Amos, Jr. founded the Famous Amos Cookie Company on March 10, 1975. After borrowing $25,000 from friends, Amos opened his first store in Hollywood. Amos' cookies were hand-baked. By 1979, the company would net $4 million in annual revenue. Major department stores such as Bloomingdale's, Neiman Marcus and Macys built partnerships with Famous Amos Cookie Company that enabled it to set up shops in their establishments. These partnerships began the trend of gourmet foods in non-food stores. Today, Famous Amos is owned by the Kellogg Company, and Amos returned to baking with Uncle Wally's Muffin Company.

Courtesy of Library of Congress Prints and Photographs Division, Washington, DC.

Marcus Mosiah Garvey

(1914)

Born in St. Ann's Bay, Jamaica, Marcus Mosiah Garvey founded the Universal Negro Improvement Association (U.N.I.A.), an international self-help organization dedicated to the uplift of people of African ancestry. Founded in 1914, the motto of the U.N.I.A. was "One God! One Aim! One Destiny." Garvey later moved to Harlem, New York where he would expand the organization's membership to over one million members while initiating other ventures. *The Negro World* was the U.N.I.A.'s weekly newspaper, founded in 1918 and published in French and Spanish as well as English. In 1919, the Black Star Line shipping company and the Negro Factories Corporation were created by Garvey and U.N.I.A members.

Robert F. Boyd

(1900s)

In the early 1900s, Robert F. Boyd, an African-American educator and doctor, opened Mercy Hospital when students and patients were no longer permitted to use the hospital near Central Tennessee College. In the 1890s, Boyd purchased a three-story brick home for $14,000. It was reportedly the largest transfer of real estate to an African-American in Tennessee.

Cirilo A. McSween

(1957)

In 1957 Cirilo A. McSween became the first African-American to represent a leading White-owned insurance company. The company was New York Life. McSween was also the first African-American to sell one million dollars worth of life insurance for a single company within one calendar year. Branching out from insurance, he joined the board of the Black-owned Independence Bank in Chicago. In 1979, Mr. McSween became the first Black business owner on the then new State Street Mall when he opened a McDonald's at 230 S. State St. He went on to own 11 more McDonald's franchises in Chicago.

The Minority Business Development Agency

(1969)

The Office of Minority Business Enterprise, later renamed The Minority Business Development Agency (MBDA), is the only agency created specifically to foster the establishment and growth of minority-owned businesses in America. In 1969, President Richard Nixon wrote Executive Order 11458 which created this government agency. The main feature of the organization and its site is to provide business consulting services to minority business owners.

Richard Spikes

(1930s)

Richard Spikes is the inventor responsible for the directional signals that have become standard in automobiles, a self-locking rack for pool cues, and the tap for beer kegs. His numerous inventions allowed Spikes to amass more than $100,000 during the 1930's, a period when few could claim the same financial security. In 1962, Spikes was completing his work on the automatic safety brake when he began to lose his vision. To complete his invention, Spikes created a drafting machine for blind designers. His safety brake is now used in school buses.

Comer J. Cottrell and James Cottrell

(1970)

Brothers Comer J. Cottrell and James Cottrell formed the Pro-Line Corporation in 1970. By 1973 he earned his first million dollars in sales. An ex-serviceman, Cottrell discovered an untapped potential for expansion through the military, as African Americans stationed overseas could not obtain hair products easily. The Air Force Exchange Service was his first customer. Cottrell has been a philanthropist and generous contributor the the HBCU Paul Quinn College. He invested in the Texas Rangers with George W. Bush, earning a $3 million profit on a $500,000 investment.

| 45 |

The East St. Louis Riots of 1917

(1917)

The East St. Louis Riots of 1917 were sparked when the Aluminum Ore Company hired nearly 500 African-American workers to replace striking White workers. White resentment turned to violence on May 28, 1917. Black men, women and children were beaten, shot and lynched by Whites. Homes of Black families were set afire. After the July 1st riot, it was estimated that between 40 and150 African-Americans lost their lives during the incidents. The NAACP and UNIA responded to the riots with investigations, protests, and rallies.

Courtesy of Library of Congress Prints and Photographs Division, Washington, DC.

Annie Malone

(1917)

In 1917, Annie Malone founded Poro College in St. Louis which employed nearly 200 people. It was dedicated to the study and teaching of Black cosmetology. In the 1890s, Malone's interest in hair textures led her to seek better hair care for Black women. By the early 1900s, Malone developed various treatments and was the first to patent the hot comb. When she became a multi-millionaire in the 1920s, she donated her money to the St. Louis Colored Orphans Home and served as its president. Today, the institution is renamed the Annie Malone Children and Family Service Center in her honor.

William R. Harvey

(1978)

William R. Harvey served as President of Hampton University for over thirty years beginning in 1978. One of his first acts upon taking the presidency of Hampton was to create a "Hampton University Market Portfolio," a group whose main focus was to raise money for the university. The group's tasks included the enlistment of corporations, foundations, and philanthropists in contributing everything from money to supplies to name recognition in order to increase Hampton's endowment and stature. In addition, he is the first African-American to own a Pepsi-Cola Bottling Company franchise.

Freddye Scarborough Henderson

(1950)

In 1950, Freddye Scarborough Henderson was the first African-American woman to receive the Master of Arts in Fashion Merchandising from the New York University School of Retailing. Henderson managed her own fashion design and custom dress design boutique in Atlanta, GA. From 1950 to 1955 Henderson was a fashion editor for the Associated Negro Press and a syndicated columnist. Henderson was also president of the National Association of Fashion and Accessory Designers. She founded Henderson Travel, the first African-American international travel agency in Atlanta and the fifth in the United States. Most notably, Henderson arranged Dr. Martin Luther King, Jr.'s travel to Norway to ccept the Nobel Peace Prize.

Clarence B. Jones

(1931)

Clarence B. Jones, born January 8, 1931, worked as personal advisor and speech-writer to Martin Luther King, Jr. However, he was also the first African-American allied member of the New York Stock Exchange (NYSE). Though Jones had voting stock in the firm as a member of the Carter, Berlind, Weill, & Levitt investment company, he did not have access to the floor. He served as a financial and legal advisor to many international governments and *Fortune* magazine honored Jones as "Man of the Month" on two different occasions.

Richard Henry Boyd

(1897)

In 1897, Richard Henry Boyd built the National Baptist Publishing Board into the largest Black-owned business of its era. The National Baptist Publishing Board became the principal source of religious publications for Black Baptists worldwide. By 1906, it was the largest African-American publishing company in the U.S. In its first 18 years, it issued more than 128 million periodicals.

New Negro Alliance (NNA)

(1933)

In 1933, the New Negro Alliance (NNA) was founded in Washington, DC to combat White-owned businesses in Black neighborhoods that would not hire Black employees. The NNA instituted a *Don't Buy Where You Can't Work* campaign to organize boycotts against such White-owned businesses. The goal was to increase job opportunities and increase awareness about collective economic power.

Anthony Overton

(1898)

Anthony Overton was the first businessman to be awarded the NAACP's Spingarn Medal. His entrepreneurship included a newspaper, *The Chicago Bee*, the Douglass National Bank, and the Victory Life Insurance Company. In 1898, with his savings of almost $2,000, he founded the Overton Hygienic Manufacturing Company, and manufactured a product he called Hygienic Pet Baking Powder. For some time he had closely followed the progress of women's cosmetics and hair products, an industry showing profits in the millions. He began to create cosmetics specifically suited for the complexions of Black women. By the time he moved his company to Chicago in 1911, his company employed a salaried sales force, as well as 400 door-to-door sales people.

DINNER GUESTS OF FERRY W. HOWARD, WHITELAW HOTEL, WASHINGTON, DC. DEC. 6 27 SCURLOCK, Photo.

Courtesy of Library of Congress Prints and Photographs Division, Washington, DC.

(1919)

Whitelaw Hotel

The Whitelaw Hotel, which opened in 1919 in Washington, DC, was the first luxury hotel for African-Americans. Jim Crow legislation and Whites-only policies made it difficult for affluent African-Americans and celebrities to find lodging in the nation's capital. Businessman John Whitelaw Lewis helped finance the building of the hotel by organizing a building association that sold stock to investors. The Whitelaw Apartment House Corporation successfully raised the $158,000 required to make the Whitelaw a reality. The hotel became a place where members of the community and performers in DC's U Street district could meet and entertain.

Willie L. Morrow

(1967)

Willie L. Morrow began researching ways to improve a cold-wave chemical treatment used to straighten hair called, "the curl." Calling it the "California Curl" in 1967, Morrow sought ways to perfect the process, and the product became an instant success earning billions of dollars for the ethnic hair care industry.

National Association for the Advancement of Colored People

(1936)

The National Association for the Advancement of Colored People (NAACP) is the nation's oldest civil rights organization, founded with a single principle – that all men and women are created equal. In 1936, The NAACP successfully sued the Montgomery County, Maryland Board of Education on behalf of William Gibbs. Gibbs was an African-American acting principal whose salary was less than that of his White counterparts. The Maryland Court of Appeals ruled in Gibbs' favor, mandating parity in the pay of county employees of all races. Following Gibbs' victory, others filed suits to end race-based discrimination in pay.

Don H. Barden

(1982)

Don H. Barden, born in 1943, established Barden Cablevision in 1982. It was both the first African-American--owned cable franchise in the United States, and the largest at that time. At its height, Barden Cablevision had 120,000 subscribers. In 1993, Barden sold his share of the company to Comcast for $300 million; he then used the money to open his first casino, the Majestic Star Riverboat, in Gary, Indiana. In 2002, Barden purchased Fitzgerald's Hotel and Casino in Las Vegas, becoming the first African-American to own a casino there.

Isaac Myers

(1866)

Isaac Myers organized and founded the Chesapeake Marine Railway and Dry Dock Company in 1866. The Baltimore, Maryland-based company was a major employee of African-American residents of the city. The company employed hundreds of caulkers, both Black and White, from all over the city. Myers went on to become the president of the Colored Caulker's Trade Union in 1868 and the Colored National Labor Union in 1869.

W. Fred Thompson

(1903)

In the early years of the twentieth century, W. Fred Thompson is believed to be the only African-American broker who worked with securities. He began his work in 1903 when African-Americans weren't allowed to participate in the industry due to discrimination and difficulty finding others who were willing to provide mentorship.

| 49 |

Christopher Gardner

(1987)

Christopher Gardner overcame personal, financial, and legal obstacles to excel in a brokerage training program so that he could land a secure position in the world of finance. Gardner began his career in Dean Witter Reynolds' stock brokerage training program, becoming a full employee in 1982 after passing his licensing exam on the first try. Eventually, Gardner became a broker for Bear Stearns & Company. In 1987, Gardner founded Gardner Rich & Company, an institutional brokerage firm specializing in the execution of debt, equity, and derivative products transactions. In 2006, "The Pursuit of Happyness," an award-winning film based on his autobiography, was released.

Courtesy of Library of Congress Prints and Photographs Division, Washington, DC.

Tulsa's Black Wall Street

(1921) Tulsa's Black Wall Street, located in the Greenwood section of Tulsa, Oklahoma, was home to a commercial district with several prominent Black businessmen, many of them multimillionaires. During the early 1900's, the buildings on Greenwood Avenue housed the offices of almost all of Tulsa's Black lawyers, realtors, doctors, and other professionals. The citizens of Tulsa had plenty of places to recycle their dollars by supporting everything from furniture stores, jewelry shops, and clothing stores to restaurants and cafes, motion picture theaters, billiard halls, and speakeasies. Seven different banks, some of which were capitalized at more than one million dollars each, were located downtown as well as offices of dozens of insurance agencies, investment advisers, accounting firms, stock and bond brokerages, real estate agencies, and loan companies. Envious whites burned Black Wall Street on May 31, 1921.

Denise Lynn Nappier

| 50 |

(1999) Both the first to serve as Connecticut's State Treasurer or in a statewide office as an African-American woman, Denise Lynn Nappier assumed office in 1999. Since then, her accomplishments include efforts to increase affordable housing for working families with the establishment of the Housing Trust Fund for Growth and Opportunity in 2005, as well as the Gift Card Law to prohibit expiration dates and inactivity fees for gift cards.

Stanley O'Neal

(2002) Stanley O'Neal became the first African-American to head a major Wall Street firm in 2002 when he took over the reins as CEO of Merrill Lynch. He joined Merrill Lynch in 1986 and rose to direct the company's leveraged finance division. As a teenager, O'Neal worked as an assembly worker for General Motors. After earning his Harvard MBA, he ascended to the position of analyst. Three years later, O'Neal became a director in General Motors' treasury division.

Napoleon Brandford III

(1997)

In 1997, Napoleon Brandford III, the youngest African-American partner on Wall Street, became the chairman of Siebert Brandford Shank, Inc., one of the largest woman and minority-owned investment banking firms in the world. Brandford founded the company with Suzanne Shank, a business partner, and Muriel Siebert, the first female NYSE seat holder. Before that, Brandford partnered with Calvin Grigsby to form Grigsby Brandford & Co. in 1985; it became one of the nation's premier investment banking firms. While there, *Ebony* named Brandford as one of its Young Tycoons in 1988.

Oseola McCarty

(1995)

Oseola McCarty earned her living as a washerwoman, and was a frugal consumer who never owned a car or subscribed to a newspaper. She was also a conservative and consistent investor. In 1995, she established a trust to provide The University of Southern Mississippi with a portion of her lifelong savings to provide scholarships for students, preferably African Americans, who need financial assistance. Given her humble circumstances, many were surprised that the amount of her bequest was about $150,000. To enhance her gift, the USM Foundation held a fund drive. Today, the Oseola McCarty Endowed Scholarship awards full-tuition scholarships to deserving students.

The Great Migration

(1923)

In 1923, The Great Migration was the period in American history when African-Americans fled the oppressive racism of the South. They relocated to the North, Midwest, and West in search of jobs and a better quality of life. In 1923, the Department of Labor published statistics attesting to the migration of half a million African-Americans. The migration of African-Americans to these regions proved to be a powerful force in the political, economic, and cultural growth of many urban areas.

| 51 |

WHUT (WHMM-TV)

(1980)

WHMM-TV began broadcasting in 1980. Now known as WHUT, the television station was the first public broadcasting station owned by African-Americans in the United States. Because WHMM was operated by Howard University, it also had the distinction of being the only television station operated by a predominantly African-American institution. In its thirty-year history, the PBS-member station has won eleven Emmys and eight Communications Excellence to Black Audiences awards. Today, the station airs PBS programming, local programs produced by Howard, and international programs focusing on Africa and the Caribbean.

Photographs and Prints Division, Schomburg Center for Research in Black Culture, The New York Public Library, Astor, Lenox and Tildan Foundation.

Sadie Tanner Mossell Alexander

(1921)

In 1921, Sadie Tanner Mossell Alexander was the first African-American woman to receive a Ph.D. in Economics from the University of Pennsylvania. Her thesis was titled *The Standard of Living among One Hundred Negro Migrant Families in Philadelphia*. Both investigative and descriptive, the work was an important documentation of the plight of such migrant families and helped draw attention to ways in which they could be helped. She was also the University of Pennsylvania Law School's first Black woman graduate and the first Black woman to be admitted to the Pennsylvania Bar. She served on President Harry Truman's Committee on Civil Rights.

Binga State Bank

(1921)

Binga State Bank was the first privately-held Black bank in the North. However, during the Great Migration in the 1900s, the bank became public. Owned and operated by Jesse Binga, the wealthiest African-American entrepreneur in 19th century Chicago, Binga State Bank offered white-collar employment opportunities for African-Americans. When Binga State Bank opened in 1921, it had deposits of $200,000. Three years later, deposits grew to over $1.3 million.

The Civil Rights Act of 1964

(1964)

The Civil Rights Act of 1964 was signed into law by President Lyndon Johnson. It prohibited all employment discrimination and established the Equal Employment Opportunity Commission to monitor any violations. Additionally, the Civil Rights Act prohibited racial discrimination in public accommodations engaged in interstate commerce. The Civil Rights Act required the withdrawal of federal funds from any institution or program that endorsed discrimination. The Civil Rights Act also ensured equal voter registration.

N. John Douglas

(1981)

In 1981, N. John Douglas founded KSTS-TV, Channel 48 in San Jose, California, the first African American-owned television station in the United States. He also served as the creator and news director of Business Today, the first nationally syndicated daily business news program to air on stations in the top five markets and on a cable network reaching six million homes. Douglas is also the founder and chairman of Douglas Broadcasting, Inc., a twenty-five station radio broadcast group created in 1989. Presently, Douglas is the president and CEO of AIM Broadcasting.

Willie Lee Wilson

(1948)

Born in 1948, Willie Lee Wilson is one of the first African-American owners of a McDonald's franchise. In 1987, Wilson started the production company Willie Wilson Productions and two years later, created and hosted Singsation! the first African-American owned and produced gospel program to appear on television. Wilson also founded Omar Medical Supplies and Gemini Electronics.

Michael Jeffrey Jordan

(1963)

Michael Jeffrey Jordan, born February 17, 1963, was elected to the NBA Hall of Fame in 2009 and is currently the majority owner of the NBA's Charlotte Bobcats. Jordan is widely considered to be the greatest basketball player of all time. As one of the most marketed sports figures in history, Jordan has been a spokesman for several internationally-known brands. Nike's "Air Jordan" brand is a $500 million business (sales), finishing last year with record profits.

| 53 |

Brown Fellowship Society

(1790)

Founded in 1790, the Brown Fellowship Society of Charleston was the first known African-American fraternal organization to encourage entrepreneurship and provide a "credit union" to support new businesses in their financing efforts. Additionally, they provided burial plots and other services. Membership in the Brown Fellowship Society was based on skin color; "brown-skinned" men were allowed to join. They could pay the $50 initiation fee while darker-skinned men were shut out. As a consequence, other fraternal organizations for darker skinned men formed. In 1893, the Brown Fellowship Society of Charleston formally changed its name to the Century Fellowship.

Courtesy of Library of Congress Prints and Photographs Division, Washington, DC.

Maida Kemp Springer

(1945) Maida Springer Kemp was one of the first African-American women to travel to Africa as a representative of the AFL-CIO in 1945. Kemp helped organize African labor unions and develop labor exchange programs and schools for workers. A pioneer in the field of international labor, Kemp worked in a garment factory shop in the United States during the 1930's. Kemp and other workers were forced to repair garments without pay, were denied lunch breaks, and had to work mandatory overtime. After joining the International Ladies Garment Workers' Union Local 22, Kemp led a strike that would end in the granting of a fifteen-dollar standard weekly wage for garment workers.

Nelson J. Edwards

(1917) Nelson J. Edwards, born in 1917, was among the first African-Americans to reach high levels of responsibility within the American Labor Movement. Edwards would eventually become the Vice-President of the United Auto Workers in 1970. He was also the first African-American to be elected to the UAW international executive board in 1962. Edwards was also a founding member of the Coalition of Black Trade Unionists (CBTU), serving as its treasurer. After his death in 1974, the CBTU created the Nelson Jack Edwards Award in his honor.

(1977) Emma Carolyn Chappell

Mentored by her pastor, Civil Rights activist Reverend Leon H. Sullivan, Emma Carolyn Chappell became the first African-American female vice president of Continental Bank in Pennsylvania in 1977. Chappell led the bank's Community Business Loan and Development Department, which was instrumental in providing loans to minority- and women-owned small businesses. She later founded the Delaware Valley Mortgage Plan, which similarly attempted to assist individual potential home owners with low and moderate incomes. Loans fell within Chappell's purview during her vice-presidency at Continental, but her idealism never led her to make bad business decisions: according to U.S. Banker, her loan-loss ratio during her twenty-year tenure was less than one percent, an impressive track record.

George E. Johnson

(1954)
___

In 1954, George E. Johnson, Sr. founded Johnson Products, a Black male hair care company. Johnson Products Company became the first Black-owned business to be listed on the American Stock Exchange. Johnson also became the first African-American to serve on Commonwealth Edison's Board of Directors. Johnson is the founder of Independence Bank.

The Birmingham Truce Agreement

(1963)
___

The Birmingham Truce Agreement stated that public facilities would be desegregated and African-Americans would be hired in the downtown shopping area. It also formed a committee to focus on solving racial problems. The agreement was reached on May 10, 1963 after a month-long protest by the Southern Christian Leadership Conference (SCLC), known as the Birmingham Campaign, with often-violent responses from the authorities. Many White-owned businesses suffered during this time due to boycotts and bad publicity; however, both business and political leaders were reluctant to meet with protestors.

George Thomas Downing

(1842)
___

George Thomas Downing opened his first restaurant and catering business in 1842 in New York. Born in 1819, Downing was an entrepreneur, caterer, and Civil Rights activist. He opened his second restaurant four years after the first one. The Oyster House opened its doors in Newport, Rhode Island in 1846. By 1850, business had grown so extensively that Downing's holdings grew into a catering enterprise. In 1854, he built the Sea Girt Hotel in Newport. The five-story hotel did not admit White clientele. Downing was also instrumental in the establishment of the Colored National Labor Union.

Brailsford R. Brazeal

(1928)
___

In 1928, Brailsford R. Brazeal was hired as an economics instructor at Morehouse College, his alma mater. By 1934 Brazeal was a professor of economics and head of the Department of Economics and Business Administration. His most recognized contribution to the field is his 1946 book, *The Brotherhood of Sleeping Car Porters, Its Origins and Development*. The book was based upon his dissertation research on the Pullman train-car porters and their successful efforts to form America's first African-American labor union. Brazeal completed his master's degree in Economics at Columbia University in 1928. He received his Ph.D. in Economics and Political Science from Columbia University in 1942.

Courtesy of Library of Congress Prints and Photographs Division, Washington, DC.

Poor People's Campaign

(1967)

The Southern Christian Leadership Conference and Dr. Martin Luther King, Jr. organized the Poor People's Campaign on December 4, 1967 to address economic issues involving poor people of every background in the U.S. The Campaign lobbied Congress to focus more on helping the poor with an anti-poverty package called the "Economic Bill of Rights." Even though it continued after King's assassination, the Campaign ended after 1968 because of Congress's lack of response. Chicago, Illinois hosted the Campaign's rebirth in 2003.

H. A. DeCosta Company

(1979)

In 1979, the H. A. DeCosta Company, a family-owned construction company, was named one of the top 100 Black-owned businesses in the nation by *Black Enterprise*. Prior to joining the family business in 1947, Herbert A. DeCosta worked as an architectural engineer for the National Advisory Committee for Aeronautics (NACA, now known as NASA). He returned to the DeCosta Company as Vice President and became President, serving there until his retirement in 1989.

H. Naylor Fitzhugh

(1933)

In 1933, H. Naylor Fitzhugh became one of the first African-Americans to receive an MBA from Harvard Business School. Despite this achievement, Fitzhugh struggled to find work in his discipline. He returned to his hometown of Washington, DC and taught marketing and management at Howard University, founding the institution's marketing program. In 1965, Fitzhugh took a marketing position with Pepsi-Cola, where his efforts to market to the African-American community ultimately landed him the position of Vice-President for Special Markets. His achievements led *Black Enterprise* magazine to dub him the "Dean of Black Business."

Gourmet Services, Inc.

(1975)

During its first year of operation in 1975, Gourmet Services, Inc. generated $2.3 million in sales. Ranked 14th out of the nation's top 50 food service companies, Gourmet Services was founded by Nathaniel Goldston III, making it one of the nation's largest Black-owned food service management companies.

Lillian Lincoln Lambert

(1969)

In 1969, Lillian Lincoln Lambert became the first African-American woman to graduate from Harvard Business School. During her first year, she, with four other Black classmates, founded the HBS African-American Student Union to increase the number of African-American students and raise scholarship money. Since graduating, Lambert founded a building management company, Centennial One, by investing $4,000 of her savings and an acquired $12,000 loan. The company launched from her own garage in Maryland in 1976. Since start up, Centennial One, Inc. has serviced clients such as ABC News, Nations-Bank and Northrop Grumman. Throughout her business career, Lambert hired 1,200 employees and accumulated annual revenues of $20 million.

Fargo Agricultural School

(1920)

Modeled after Booker T. Washington's philosophy of education and the labor opportunities for Black Southerners of the day, Floyd Brown, a Tuskegee Institute alum, founded the Fargo Agricultural School in 1920. He purchased 20 acres of land, and the school was built with donations of money and labor. Fargo's curriculum was two-fold: half of the day was dedicated to academic studies (English, math, history, music, and natural sciences), while the other half of the day was dedicated to job training. The girls learned home economics while the boys learned skills such as tool repair and carpentry. Brown himself taught a practical reasoning class he called the "Class in Common Sense."

Jan Matzeliger

(1883)

Jan Matzeliger invented and patented the shoe-lasting machine in 1883. The invention allowed shoes to be produced more efficiently, resulting in a 50% reduction in overhead. This resulted in doubled wages and improved working conditions for those employed by the industry. Matzeliger later sold his patent to Sydney W. Winslow.

Courtesy of Library of Congress Prints and Photographs Division, Washington, DC.

Southern Tenant Farmers Union

(1934) The Southern Tenant Farmers' Union (STFU) was founded in Tyronza, Arkansas in 1934. Organized in the Depression-era South by Black agricultural laborers, STFU was initially established to protest the eviction of 23 farm families and sharecroppers from land they had worked for years. As enrollment continued to increase, land owners began to harass and evict their tenants. Congress responded with the creation of the Farm Security Administration (FSA) in the fall of 1936. As part of the FSA, the Farm Security Corporation was established, providing loans to poor farmers in an effort to enable them to purchase their own land.

Joseph A. Pierce

(1947) Joseph A. Pierce's *Negro Business and Business Education* was published in 1947. The book was the result of a study Pierce conducted from 1944 to 1946. Jointly sponsored by the National Urban League and Atlanta University, the study was also supported by twenty African-American universities and colleges throughout the South. The purpose of the study was to investigate the presence of African-American--owned business and the opportunities for increasing the number of them in twelve U.S. cities. Pierce was a staunch advocate of business education for African-Americans and believed prevailing attitudes and existing laws could be beneficial to African-Americans.

Dr. Robert Weaver

(1966) Economist Dr. Robert Weaver was the nation's first African-American Cabinet secretary. He led the Department of Housing and Urban Development from 1966 until 1969. In the late 1950s, Weaver was New York State's Rent Commissioner. In 1960, he became Vice Chairman of the New York City Housing and Redevelopment Board. President-elect Kennedy asked Weaver to serve as the administrator of the Housing and Home Finance Agency (HHFA). In that capacity, Weaver helped author the 1961 compilation housing bill and supported the 1962 Senior Citizens Housing Act. Weaver worked on the $7.8 billion housing bill in 1965 which included an expansion of public housing and programs for rent supplementation for low-income families.

FUBU

(1992)

Daymond John, J. Alexander, Keith Perrin, and Carl Brown began the FUBU line in 1992, initially starting with hats, and then broadening their line to men's, women's, and children's fashions. At its peak, FUBU grossed $350 million in annual worldwide sales, and in 1995, Samsung invested in the company, helping with distribution.

The Comprehensive Employment and Training Act of 1973

(1973)

The Comprehensive Employment and Training Act of 1973 (CETA) was a successful piece of legislation that helped offset the large numbers of unemployed African-Americans. CETA furnished job training programs, and to the extent possible, jobs for the chronically unemployed. While CETA was not specifically designed for African-Americans, because they represented such a large percentage of the nation's unemployed citizens, much of the programming was directed towards this community. Criticism from influential conservatives and a lackluster economy contributed to the termination of CETA in 1981.

Blanche K. Bruce

(1874)

Elected on February 4, 1874, former slave Blanche K. Bruce became a United States Senator. Appointed by President Garfield in 1881, Bruce would serve as Register of the United States Treasury for over a decade. Subsequently, his signature appeared on U.S. currency, making this feat an African-American first. Bruce operated a successful business in Washington, DC, handling investments, claims, insurance, and real estate. In 1893, Bruce received an honorary LL.D. and joined the board of trustees at Howard University. Before serving as a Senator, he was a wealthy landowner in the Mississippi Delta.

| 59 |

Women's Day on Wall Street

(1957)

To lure women into the stock market, Wilhelmina B. Drake created "Women's Day on Wall Street" in 1957. Drake served three important positions: Director of Women's Activities, member of the board of directors and corporate secretary of Special Markets, Inc. She focused the "Women's Day on Wall Street" event on the benefits of investing, including saving for children's education, as well as a home, business, traveling or retirement.

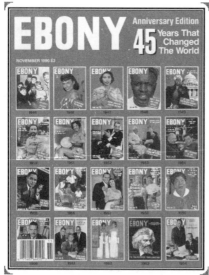

Courtesy of Ebony Magazine.

Johnson Publishing Company

(1942) In 1942, John H. Johnson launched *Negro Digest.* Patterned after *Reader's Digest,* Johnson's magazine was created with a focus on issues of interest to the African-American community. Building upon the success of his first magazine, Johnson next launched *Ebony,* a lifestyle magazine for African-Americans that was modeled after *Life* magazine. Johnson's empire expanded to include *Jet* magazine and continues today. The company also has a book division, a cosmetics line (Fashion Fair), and a line of hair care products (Supreme Beauty). Johnson Publishing Company has more than 300 full-time employees and annual sales that exceeded $480 million in 2003.

Xernona Clayton

(1968) Xernona Clayton was the first Black woman in the South to host a regular primetime television talk show, Variations, on WAGA-TV in Atlanta in 1968. The show was later renamed The Xernona Clayton Show. Guests included Harry Belafonte and Lena Horne. Clayton also organized fundraising events for the Southern Christian Leadership Conference, working directly with Dr. Martin Luther King, Jr. and Mrs. Coretta Scott King. In her early career, Clayton worked as an undercover agent for Chicago's Urban League. She investigated employment discrimination along with her twin sister. As a result of one of their investigations, one of the companies they probed, a liquor distribution firm, offered them jobs, which was a first in the company's history.

Robert P. Madison International, Inc.

(1954) Robert P. Madison International, Inc. was the tenth African-American-- owned architectural firm in the nation, but it was Cleveland, Ohio's first. The firm was established in 1954 by Cleveland native Robert P. Madison. In 1957, the Cleveland Chamber of Commerce selected the Mt. Pleasant Medical Center, one of the firm's designs, as one of the ten best buildings constructed in Cleveland. Madison International was selected by many prestigious clients, from the U.S. State Department to Tuskegee Institute, along with the nations of Trinidad and Tobago, Jamaica, The Bahamas, and Nigeria.

Johnny Mack Brown

(1970)

Johnny Mack Brown, born in 1943, was the first African-American, and fifth independent, Goodyear dealer. Born in rural Alabama to a sharecropper father and a mother who worked as a domestic, Brown was one of twelve children. The Brown children worked in the cotton fields during the 1960s. After the death of his father, Brown and his brothers began to save money so they might be able to provide for their mother. When the local Goodyear tire dealership where Brown worked began to falter, Brown purchased it. In 1970, the dealership reopened as Johnny Brown's Tire Company.

The Negro as Capitalist and The Black Worker

(1899)

Abram Lincoln Harris, Jr., born January 17, 1899, authored *The Negro as Capitalist, 1936* and *The Black Worker, 1931*. In *The Black Worker,* Harris states that African-Americans should end racial antagonism in the working class and suggested that they learn more about unionism and its benefits since many moved to the North for economic opportunities. In *The Negro Capitalist,* Harris addressed the growing anti-business sentiment of the Great Depression and stated that African-American businessmen were under a false sense of racial solidarity between the Blacks and the Whites. He suggested that African-Americans need to participate in trade unionism with White businessmen and concluded that business can't grow unless there is interracial trade.

Grafton Tyler Brown

(1867)

In 1867, Grafton Tyler Brown founded G.T. Brown and Company, which produced fine designs for stock certificates and lithographs of California towns. Brown, a painter, lithographer, draftsman, engineer, and entrepreneur is considered the first professional African-American artist in California. Brown began his career as a draftsman for the firm of Kucheland and Dressel.

Weeksville

(1838)

In 1838, a section of Brooklyn, New York, Weeksville was founded from land purchased by Black freedmen Henry C. Thompson and James Weeks. Weeksville became the second largest independent Black community in pre-Civil War America. Approximately one-third of Weeksville's male residents over the age of 21 owned land in the community. More than 500 of Weeksville's residents came from all over the East Coast, two of which, were African-born. During the New York Draft Riot, Weeksville became a refuge for African-Americans who fled Manhattan.

Courtesy of Library of Congress Prints and Photographs Division, Washington, DC.

Motown Records

(1959) In Detroit, Michigan, Berry Gordy, Jr. founded Motown Record Company, or Motown, as it is commonly known, in 1959. It was the first African-American --owned music company to achieve crossover success in America. Motown gained local success and secured national recognition with singles from two of its earliest musical groups. In 1960, the Miracles released "Shop Around," which was followed by The Marvelettes' "Please Mister Postman" in 1961. Vaulted into the national spotlight, Motown continued its meteoric rise. Today, the company is owned by Universal Music Group. Gordy's estimated net worth is a half billion dollars.

Milton Davis

(1973) Milton Davis was the co-founder of the nation's first development bank, Shore Bank Corporation. When the bank began to fail, Davis and his associates bought it in 1973. The bank was made viable in five years. Milton Davis, James Fletcher, Mary Houghton, and Ron Grzywinski purchased the bank after successfully petitioning the federal Comptroller of the Currency. They bought the struggling South Shore National Bank with $800,000 in capital and a $2.4 million bank loan. In 2000, the name was officially changed to ShoreBank. ShoreBank is the leading bank holding company committed to increasing economic opportunities for underserved urban and rural communities.

Oprah Winfrey

(1986) In 1986, Oprah Winfrey's nationally-syndicated talk show debuted. The "Oprah Winfrey Show" went on to win many awards and was named the highest-rated program of its kind in history. In 1986, Winfrey founded Harpo Productions, Inc., a multimedia production company which houses Harpo Studios, Harpo Radio, Inc., and Harpo Films, Inc. She also publishes *O, The Oprah Magazine* and *O at Home,* and in 2011 will launch her own cable channel, the Oprah Winfrey Network. With a 2000 net worth of $800 million, Winfrey is believed to be the richest African-American of the 20th century.

James Garfield Beck

(1913)

In 1913, James Garfield Beck became the first African-American postal clerk in Tennessee. His wife, Ethel Benson Beck headed the Knoxville Colored Orphanage. She was instrumental in building a $10,000 brick building. The orphanage was later renamed the Ethel Beck Home for Children in her honor. The Becks were two of the most influential members of Knoxville's Black community of the 1920's, 30's, and 40's.

MacFarlane Partners

(1987)

MacFarlane Partners, an investment management firm specializing in real estate founded by Victor MacFarlane in 1987, found its big break in 1995 when they teamed up with Magic Johnson to revitalize L.A. neighborhoods destroyed in the riots with $50 million from the California Public Employee Retirement System. MacFarlane's projects aimed to rebuild inner-city shopping centers and return large profits, and in 2008, MacFarlane Partners was named the #1 private equity firm in *Black Enterprise*.

Charles Richard Patterson

(1915)

The C.R. Patterson & Son Carriage Company of Greenfield, Ohio became the world's first and only automobile manufacturing company founded and owned by African-Americans. Founded by Charles Richard Patterson in 1915, the company began as a manufacturer of horse-drawn carriages and ended up as a manufacturer of buses. The company produced the Patterson-Greenfield which was the first car made by an African-American automaker.

Bettiann Gardner

(1964)

In 1964, Bettiann Gardner and her husband Edward launched the hair care business Soft Sheen from the basement of their Chicago, Illinois home. Soft Sheen would grow to become a multi-million dollar enterprise, employing more than 400 residents from throughout the city of Chicago. Due to the popularity of products such as the Care Free Curl and Optimum Care lines, revenue in 1989 was up to $87.2 million. In 1997, the total in sales was $94.5 million. In 1998, cosmetics giant L'Oreal purchased the company.

Courtesy of Library of Congress Prints and Photographs Division, Washington, DC.

Arthur George (A.G.) Gaston

(1923)

Arthur George (A.G.) Gaston was one of the most influential entrepreneurs of the twentieth century. In 1923, Gaston founded his first business, the Booker T. Washington Burial Society. The society's success led to the establishment of the Booker T. Washington Insurance Company, which offered life, health, and accident insurance to its customers. Due to the shortage of skilled office workers in his businesses, he founded the Booker T. Washington Business College in 1939. Gaston continued to grow his business empire with the addition of the Vulcan Realty and Investment Company, A.G. Gaston Home for Senior Citizens, WENN-FM and WAGG-AM radio stations, S & G Public Relations Company, A.G. Gaston Motel, and Citizens Federal Savings and Loan Association.

Christopher F. Edley, Sr.

(1973)

Christopher F. Edley, Sr. served as President of the United Negro College Fund (UNCF) from 1973 to 1990. While leading UNCF, Edley raised $700 million through events such as the annual "Lou Rawls' Parade of Stars," now called "An Evening of Stars: A Celebration of Educational Excellence." He also raised $50 million through a challenge grant from *TV Guide* founder and former diplomat Walter H. Annenberg. This was the largest gift in Black philanthropic history.

WLIB-AM

(1971)

In 1971, WLIB-AM became the first African-American--owned radio station in New York City when the Inner City Broadcasting Company, co-founded by African-American lawyer and businessman Percy Sutton, bought the station. Born in 1920, Sutton was a mentor and pioneer in the business, government, and legal sectors. In 1995, he served as a member of an American delegation of businessmen representing the United States at the G-7 roundtable meeting on Telecommunications and High Technology. Sutton orchestrated the refurbishing and reopening of the historic Apollo Theater in Harlem. Until his death in 2009, Sutton continued to support political, business, and communication ventures in the community.

Webb & Brooker, Inc.

(1968)

Eugene Webb and George Brooker founded Webb & Brooker, Inc. in 1968 as a real estate management brokerage firm in Harlem. Now, over forty years later, Webb & Brooker, Inc. continues to be one of the most successful real estate firms in Harlem, accumulating a large amount of commercial and residential properties throughout the newly-revitalized Harlem and greater New York Metro areas.

The True Reformers Savings Bank

(1907)

The True Reformers Savings Bank, the first Black bank in America to receive a charter, acquired more than $1 million deposits in 1907. The bank was founded by former slave turned minister, William Washington Browne, who urged the formation of "fountains" to pool money to purchase land. Browne traveled throughout parts of the South establishing local chapters, called sub-fountains, addressing issues like commercial insurance companies charging African-American customers higher rates than Whites. This African-American fraternal organization not only offered life insurance, but also organized the first Black-owned bank in the United States. The Order also owned a hotel, retail stores, and a newspaper.

Daniels & Bell, Inc.

(1971)

June 24, 1971, Daniels & Bell, Inc. is the first African-American--owned securities firm to purchase a New York Stock Exchange (NYSE) member seat. Travers J. Bell and Willie Daniels founded the firm with $170,000 in capital. Although Daniels & Bell struggled during its first years, buying a seat on the NYSE helped raise its profile. In 1986, Daniels & Bell ranked 20th among the top municipal financial business. However, the company lost its membership in 1999 after a steep and steady decline following Bell's death in 1988.

| 65 |

Smith Graham & Company

(1990)

Gerald Smith and Ladell Graham founded Smith Graham & Company in 1990, the largest African-American firm dealing with fixed-income asset management. When Smith Graham & Company sold 40% of the firm to the Robeco Group in the Netherlands in 1996, it became the only African-American firm with overseas influence.

Courtesy of Dr. Julianne Malveaux.

Phyllis Ann Wallace

(1965)

Born in 1923, Phyllis Ann Wallace was the first African-American and female president of the Industrial Relations Research Association. In 1965, as the Chief of Technical Studies for the Equal Employment Opportunity Commission (EEOC), Wallace researched race and the labor market. Professor Wallace spearheaded, through her scholarship, a precedent-setting legal decision in a federal case that reversed sex and race discrimination in American industry. She directed studies for the federal lawsuit against American Telephone and Telegraph Co., then the largest private employer in the United States. The suit led to a 1973 decision that the company had discriminated against both women and minority men.

WHUR-FM

(1971)

In 1971, Howard University's WHUR-FM began broadcasting in Washington, DC. The radio station, a gift to the university from the Washington Post Company, was the first African-American--owned station to air in the Washington, DC metropolitan area. WHUR's staff also serves as mentors for students attending Howard University's School of Communications. Today, it is the Washington area's only stand-alone radio station, one of just a few university-owned commercial radio stations in the U.S. WHUR is the first Washington-area radio station to broadcast in High Definition (HD).

Ben's Chili Bowl

(1958)

Ben's Chili Bowl opened in 1958 on Washington, DC's U Street Corridor, which was also known as "Black Broadway." The restaurant, owned by the late Ben Ali and his wife Virginia, became a mainstay in the area. Using $5,000, the newly-wedded couple renovated a silent movie theater turned pool hall into their restaurant space. Ben's Chili Bowl survived riots and economic change and is still in operation in the same location today. It is one of DC's historical landmarks. In recent years, the restaurant expanded by opening a restaurant and bar next door called Ben's Next Door.

Russell Goings

(1968)

In 1968, Russell Goings became the first African-American manager for Shearson Hammill, Inc.'s Harlem Branch, later bought by Goings who changed its name to First Harlem Securities. The firm eventually became one of the first Black-owned brokerage firms to own a seat in the NYSE.

Maynard H. Jackson

(1973)

Maynard H. Jackson became the first Black mayor in a major capital city of the South, Atlanta, on Oct. 16, 1973. Jackson has been lauded for making Atlanta a distribution hub, convention destination, and financial center. Under his leadership, Atlanta built the world's largest airport. One of Mayor Jackson's main priorities was to ensure that minority businesses received more municipal contracts, and he succeeded in raising the proportion from less than 1 percent to more than 35 percent.

Black Expo

(1971)

In 1971, Chicago, Illinois hosted the first Black Expo. Heralded as the largest gathering of Black businessmen in history, the expo showcased the wares of more than 350 African-American businesses. This five-day event provided a venue for African-American business owners to make vital connections with potential customers from the private sector, the general public, and government agencies. Booths representing the businesses in attendance allowed entrepreneurs to exhibit their products and services to a targeted audience. This increased exposure supported the growth of African-American businesses and is part of a tradition that continues in cities across the nation today.

Garland Wood

(1986)

Goldman Sachs, a global investment banking and securities firm, welcomed Garland Wood as its first African-American partner in 1986. Wood came to Goldman Sachs from Columbia University, where he earned an undergraduate degree in economics and an MBA. In 1976, he was promoted to vice president, and 10 years later he became a partner.

Courtesy of Library of Congress Prints and Photographs Division, Washington, DC.

March on Washington

(1963) With labor, religious, and Civil Rights leaders, Martin Luther King, Jr. helped organize the August 28, 1963 March on Washington for Jobs and Freedom. His famous "I Have a Dream" speech referenced the Constitution and Declaration of Independence and claimed they were promissory notes to the "inalienable rights" of "life, liberty and the pursuit of happiness." King stated that America had given African-Americans a bad check, returned due to "insufficient funds." Refusing to believe that there is a problem of insufficient funds in America, King rallied the audience with his words, "We have come to our nation's capital to cash a check."

William McDonald Felton

(1910) In 1910, William McDonald Felton opened an auto dealership and repair shop. *The New York Age*, an African-American newspaper, claimed Felton's Auto Transportation and Sales Company was "the largest automobile business conducted by Negroes in New York." Felton also opened the Automobile and Aeroplane Mechanical School in Harrisburg, Pennsylvania in 1923. The two-story school building, which cost $100,000 to build, offered training for operating and repairing cars and planes while both were still being introduced. To expand his business, Felton advertised for mechanical correspondence courses as far away as Chicago.

Parks Sausage Company

(1970) In 1970, the Parks Sausage Company became the first African-American--owned business to be publicly held on the NASDAQ stock market. The company was founded in 1951 and owned by Henry G. Parks, Jr., a graduate of Ohio State University's marketing program. Within the first three months of operation, the company grossed $30,000. In 1952, Parks hired a new General Manager. New products and sales were added, and by 1990 the company had even relocated. In its high point, the company made $30 million and employed 250 people.

Willard Townsend, Jr.

(1895)

Willard Townsend, Jr. was an African-American labor leader born in Cincinnati, Ohio in 1895. He initially worked as a redcap for the railroads before earning a degree in Chemistry from the Royal College of Science, University of London. Townsend later found work in the railways of Chicago, Illinois. Dissatisfied with the infrequent pay African-Americans received, and their dependence on tips, Townsend chose to organize a union. The Labor Auxiliary of Redcaps was established in 1937 to get redcaps recognized as employees and granted them rights to negotiate better pay and working conditions.

The United Negro College Fund

(1944)

Established as a corporation in 1944, The United Negro College Fund serves as the nation's largest and most comprehensive minority higher education assistance organization. In 63 years, it has raised over $2 billion to assist more than 350,000 students. UNCF's mission is to close the educational attainment gap between African-Americans and the majority population. UNCF enables over 50,000 students a year attend college. The United Negro College Fund has distributed more funds to assist in the education of minorities than any other entity outside of the federal government.

Janice Bryant Howroyd

(1978)

Janice Bryant Howroyd is the founder and CEO of Act One Personnel Services, a company that has provided staffing solutions for corporations nationwide since 1978. From an initial investment of $1,500, her company is now one of the largest owned by an African-American in the United States. Today, the employment services agency generates annual revenues approaching $1 billion.

| 69 |

North Carolina Mutual and Provident Insurance Company

(1898)

In 1898, John Merrick, Charles Clinton Spaulding and Dr. Aaron McDuffe Moore founded North Carolina Mutual and Provident Insurance Company in Durham, North Carolina. Each person contributed $50 to buy shares and Merrick served as its first president. Its premium income grew from $840 in 1899 to $1,224,541 in 1919. The company employed over 1,200 people in January of 1920. By 1948, North Carolina Mutual and Provident Insurance Company was the largest African-American owned business in the country. Operating in 24 states plus Washington, DC today, the company enjoys assets of $210 million, a surplus of $26.2 million, and an insurance force of $1.4 billion.

Courtesy of Library of Congress Prints and Photographs Division, Washington, DC.

Augustus Hawkins

(1962)

Augustus Hawkins, the first Black representative from any western state, was elected to Congress in 1962 from the state of California. Early in his political career, California Assemblyman Hawkins introduced a number of acts including ones for fair housing, fair employment practices, low-cost housing, disability insurance legislation, and workmen's compensation provisions for domestic workers. As a Congressman, Hawkins' most popular legislative work was The Humphrey-Hawkins Act of 1978, also known as the Full Employment and Balanced Growth Act.

The National Association of Negro Business and Professional Women's Clubs

(1936)

The National Association of Negro Business and Professional Women's Clubs held its first convention in Atlantic City, NJ in 1936. It was founded by owners, managers, college graduates and other professionally-licensed women as a national organization for women of high caliber in hopes of encouraging others to organize similar clubs within their communities. Club members shared experiences and exchanged information to encourage and develop opportunities for Black women in business professions

Albert W. Johnson

(1971)

Albert W. Johnson was the first African-American to purchase a General Motors franchise. He became one of the most successful independent Cadillac dealers in the nation. In 1971, he started selling Cadillacs at a dealership in the South Shore neighborhood, which six years later he moved to Tinley Park. Mr. Johnson sold his dealership in 1994. Johnson started selling cars in St. Louis in 1953, later moving to an Oldsmobile dealership in Kirkwood, Mo., where he was known as "the man who sold cars from a briefcase," since he wasn't allowed to sell inside of the dealership due to his skin color.

Lonnie G. Johnson and Bruce D'Andrade

(1989)

Lonnie G. Johnson and Bruce D'Andrade are best known for creating a prototype of the Super Soaker™ in 1989. With over 40 million sold, the Super Soaker™ has generated over $200 million in sales. Prior to his Super Soaker™ success, Johnson worked to develop thermodynamic and control systems for NASA's Jet Propulsion Laboratory, most notably for the Galileo Jupiter probe and the Mars Observer project.

Marvin Early Perry

(1984)

In 1984, Marvin Early Perry founded the Black Board of Directors Project in Phoenix, Arizona. The project's aims were to address the dearth of African-Americans and other under-represented minorities serving as board members of corporate, charitable, and public policy organizations. In the organization's twenty-six year history, the Black Board of Directors Project has placed over 2,000 Blacks and other minorities on various boards and commissions. By facilitating seminars and conferences centered on corporate board education, Perry's goal is to empower members of Arizona's Black community by encouraging them to seek board membership on a corporate level. In doing so, local businesses and agencies will involve more minorities in their policy-making processes.

Lamond Godwin

(1981)

Lamond Godwin was named Secretary of Labor for Operation PUSH in 1981. At this point, Godwin served under President Carter as the director of national programs for the Employment and Training Administration in the Department of Labor. In 1994, Godwin, chairman and chief executive, founded a portfolio management company, Peachtree Asset Management.

Otis Boykin

(1961)

Electronic scientist, inventor, and designer Otis Boykin invented the heart pacemaker and received a patent for it on February 21, 1961. He also patented an electronic resistor, a revolutionary innovation that is used in radios, computers, televisions, and other electronic devices. Boykin's resistor helped reduce the cost of those electronics. He patented over twenty electronic devices throughout his career. Boykin also founded Boykin-Fruth, Inc. in the mid 1940's.

Photographs and Prints Division, Schomburg Center for Research in Black Culture, The New York Public Library, Astor, Lenox and Tildan Foundation.

Andrew Brimmer

(1966)

In 1966, Dr. Andrew F. Brimmer was the first African-American to serve on the Federal Reserve Board. First and foremost an economist, Brimmer promoted a monetary policy that sought to alleviate unemployment and reduce the national deficit. He also argued that racial discrimination hurt the U.S economy by marginalizing potentially productive workers. In 1963, President John F. Kennedy appointed Brimmer as Deputy Assistant Secretary of Commerce for Economic Policy and then Assistant Secretary for Economic Affairs. In 1966, he was appointed to the Board of Governors for the Federal Reserve Bank by President Lyndon B. Johnson.

The Southern Negro Youth Congress

(1936)

The Southern Negro Youth Congress (SNYC) supported young African-Americans engaged in the struggle for social justice, economic and political parity, and full Black citizenship. It was formed by the young people who had attended the National Negro Congress (NNC) in Chicago, IL in 1936. Its headquarters were initially established in Richmond, VA before moving to Birmingham, AL in 1939. Its first conference was held on February 13-14, 1937. One of SNYC's early campaign successes included a protest in support of Black tobacco workers' actions in opposing poor wages and hazardous working conditions in Richmond, Virginia.

John Edward Bush

(1856)

John Edward Bush, a former slave born in 1856, began to show entrepreneurial talent at age 19, when he purchased a city lot for $150. The lot was later sold at a profit that allowed him to purchase three new properties. Bush established the Mosaic Templars in 1882 in Little Rock, Arkansas. The Templars provided members insurance for illness, death and burial. At the time, these services were not traditionally afforded to African-Americans at that time. By 1918, the Templars became an international organization, with chapters in Central America and the West Indies. There were at least 80,000 members with assets exceeding $300,000.

John Jones

(1816)

John Jones, born in 1816, was thought by many to be the most affluent African-American in the Midwest of his era. His Clothes Cleaning and Repairing Rooms enterprise (formerly known as J. Jones, Clothes Dresser and Repairer), a cleaning and tailoring shop he started in March 1845, catered to Chicago's most important residents. The shop earned Jones between $85,000 and $100,000; a fortune at the time. Although Jones lost money in the Great Chicago Fire of 1871, he was still recognized as one of the richest African-Americans in the country.

Clifton R. Wharton

(1987)

Clifton R. Wharton was the first African American to receive the Ph.D. in economics from the University of Chicago. He had careers in philanthropy, foreign service, higher education leadership, and corporate America. In 1987, he became CEO the Teacher's Insurance and Annuity Association – College Equities Fund (TIAA-CREF), the first African-American to head a major US corporation. He served on several corporate boards, including Ford Motor Company, Time Warner, Equitable Life, and the New York Stock Exchange.

Asa Timothy Spaulding

(1902)

Asa Timothy Spaulding, who was born in 1902, served as President of the North Carolina Mutual Life Insurance Company from 1959 until 1967. Before serving as president, Spaulding served the company as assistant secretary, vice president, actuary & controller, and director. Spaulding was the first African-American actuary or professional statistician to work for an insurance company. He also served in various positions with other enterprises, including Mechanics and Farmers Bank, Winston Mutual Life Insurance Company, Dunbar Life Insurance Company, Mutual Savings and Loan Association and Realty Services, Inc.

| 73 |

Ron Brown

(1993)

In 1993, President William Jefferson Clinton appointed Ron Brown as the first African-American Secretary of Commerce. As commerce secretary, Brown won praise for breathing new life into the department. He revived its export programs, winning lucrative multibillion-dollar contracts for U.S. aircraft and telecommunications firms. He also presided over a $900 million annual budget for promoting high technology in small and medium-sized business, nearly double the amount spent during the administration of George Bush. *The New Republic* called him "the most formidable Commerce secretary since Herbert Hoover."

Courtesy of Library of Congress Prints and Photographs Division, Washington, DC.

Fannie Lou Hamer

(1968)

In 1968, Fannie Lou Hamer created Pig Banks, a rural cooperative that provided livestock for poor people in Mississippi. Under the leadership of Dr. Dorothy Height, the National Council of Negro Women contributed pigs to participating families who were then trained to care for pigs, establish cooperatives, and work together to improve the community's nutrition and health. The following year, Hamer established Freedom Farm with a similar goal of providing food and some economic independence for local people. These projects were critical to the economic development of southern rural communities as well as having a positive impact in terms of education and political empowerment.

Chester Franklin

(1880)

Chester Franklin, born in 1880, began his career in the newspaper business at age 17 when he assumed leadership of his father's newspaper, *The Star*. Later, Franklin founded *The Call* in Kansas City. Franklin trained men and women in all facets of the newspaper business. With the help of his wife and mother, Chester Franklin developed one of the best newspapers in the Midwest. *The Call* was also a source of influence in the fight for civil rights; through the newspaper, Blacks learned of efforts to reduce segregation in housing and jobs. At one point, Roy Wilkins, who was editor during the 1920s and 1930s, called for boycotting a bakery because they didn't hire African-Americans as delivery drivers.

Franklin Augustine Thomas

(1967)

As President of the Bedford-Stuyvesant Restoration Corporation from 1967-1977, Franklin Augustine Thomas raised more than $62 million in public and private funds to increase the development of businesses, jobs and housing in his home community. He served as President of the Ford Foundation from 1979 until 1996, its first African American leader. When he resigned, the foundation had $7.7 billion in assets, making it one of the nation's largest philanthropic organizations.

Memphis Sanitation Strike

(1968)

In 1968, when AFSCME Local 1733 went on strike to obtain raises and the right to bargain, its 1,300 workers endured a bitter 65-day struggle. Known as the Memphis Sanitation Strike, this action was prompted by two deaths (Echol Cole and Robert Walker) which happened due to the mistreatment, discrimination, and dangerous working environment endured by Black sanitation workers. This sanitation strike attracted national media attention, particularly after the much revered Dr. Martin Luther King, Jr. took an active role in it. The assassination of Dr. King on April 4th was credited in helping to influence the favorable strike settlement that was reached a week later.

(1822) ### William Ellison

By the time William Ellison founded his manufacturing company in 1822, he had long been recognized as a successful cotton gin repairer and manufacturer. His contribution to the improved design of the cotton gin raised his already prominent position in society. Born a slave, Ellison was to become one of the richest African-Americans in the South. It is believed that, outside of the state of Louisiana, Ellison may have been the richest African-American of his time.

Nathan G. Conyers

(1970)

Nathan G. Conyers, born in 1932, was the owner and founder of Conyers Riverside Ford, the only Black-owned dealership in Detroit, and the oldest Black-owned dealership in the nation. Conyers organized the National Bank Dealers Association in 1970. With the assistance of the Reverend Jesse Jackson, Conyers helped forge the National Black Dealers Association and became its first president in 1970. In 1979, Conyers established the Ford Lincoln Mercury Black Dealers Association. In May of that same year, minority dealers met with the goal of leveraging much needed financial support from federal agencies. As a result of this effort, the National Minority Dealership Association was formed.

| 75 |

Barbara Proctor

(1970)

Barbara Proctor started her own advertising company in 1970, believing in the African-American market. Proctor and Gardner Advertising, Inc. now has many high-profile clients and is one of the largest ad agencies headed by an African-American in the United States. Her clients include Jewel Foods and Sears, Roebuck and Company to mention a few.

Library of Congress Prints and Photographs Division, Washington, DC.

Black "Rosie the Riveters"

(1943)

World War II production requirements pulled women, first white, and then African American into the paid labor force in unprecedented numbers. This photo of an African American working on the Vultee A-31 Vengeance dive bomber at the Vultee plant in Nashville, Tennessee in 1943 symbolizes the Black "Rosie the Riveters", women who worked in traditionally male jobs because their work was needed for the war effort. The number of women in the paid labor market increased by 57 percent between 1940 and 1944.

Phillis Wheatley

(1753)

Born in West Africa around 1753 and brought to Boston, MA in 1761 as a slave, Phillis Wheatley was tutored in English, Latin, history, geography, and the Bible. Wheatley went on to publish her first poem in 1767 in the *Newport Mercury* titled, "On Messrs. Hussey and Coffin." Wheatley also authored *Poems on Various Subjects, Religious and Moral,* the first book of poetry by an African-American. The book was published in London.

Herman Petty

(1968)

The first African-American--owned McDonald's franchise was opened by Herman Petty in 1968 in Chicago, Illinois. By the end of 1969, there were twelve African-American--owned McDonald's restaurants. McDonald's first African-American field consultant met with the operators and managers from each of these franchises, building the foundation upon which the National Black McDonald's Operators Association (NBMOA) was created. The first NBMOA convention was held in May 1972, bringing together twelve founding members and five company leaders. Today, the NBMOA have members who own at least 1,300 McDonald's throughout the United States, South Africa, and the Caribbean with annual sales of memberships exceeding $3 billion.

Kansas Exodus

(1879)

After the Civil War, and during the years of Reconstruction, thousands of African-Americans fled west to Kansas to escape poor living conditions and disenfranchisement in the South. During the mass exodus, leaders such as Benjamin "Pap" Singleton established settlements and businesses in Kansas, Oklahoma, and Colorado. Although it was short-lived, the Kansas Exodus in 1879 did expose the plight of African-American workers.

Montgomery Bus Boycott

(1955)

Beginning in 1955, the Montgomery Bus Boycott was one of the defining events of the Civil Rights Movement. The boycott was supported by most of Montgomery's 40,000 Black residents. The Montgomery Improvement Association created a highly efficient carpool system managed by women leaders. This effort had a significant and negative financial impact on the city's bus company.

Ernesta Procope

(1979)

Ernesta Procope, founder, President and Chief Executive Office of EG Bowman Company, grew her business from a small insurance company to the first minority-owned brokerage firm on Wall Street. Intially housed in Bedford Styvesant, Brooklyn, New York, in 1979 the private investment firm relocated to 97 Wall Street. Procope started her firm in 1953 as a direct response to the denial of coverage to African-American communities. Procope informed her clients that the commercial value of property was a direct connection to building wealth.

| 77 |

The National Coalition of Blacks for Reparations in America

(1987)

The National Coalition of Blacks for Reparations in America's (N'COBRA) founding meeting was held in 1987 for the purpose of broadening the reparations movement's base of support. N'COBRA is an international coalition of organizations and individuals committed to the economic, cultural, intellectual, political, social, and spiritual empowerment of Black people in the USA. N'COBRA's motto: "We want our just inheritance: the trillions of dollars due us for the labor of our ancestors who worked for hundreds of years without pay."

Photographs and Prints Division, Schomburg Center for Research in Black Culture, The New York Public Library, Astor, Lenox and Tildan Foundation.

Robert S. Browne

(1969)

The Black Economic Research Center was founded by Robert S. Browne in 1969 and became a center of applied research that generated the services of Black economists for Black development projects. Browne published and served as a director of *The Review of Black Political Economy* until 1980. In addition to his directorial endeavors, Browne also founded and organized the Emergency Land Fund (ELF) to address the cause of African-American land loss. The ELF received funds from the Department of Agriculture to conduct research on heir property in the southern Black community.

Philip A. Payton, Jr.

(1904)

Philip A. Payton, Jr.'s real estate company, the Afro-American Realty Company, was chartered in 1904. It was capitalized at $50,000. Payton sought to erase the color line in Harlem, then an up-scale, all-White neighborhood, by placing Black families in apartments. By 1905, it had assets valued at over $600,000 and controlled twenty New York apartment houses. Payton's early work consisted of being a handyman at six dollars a week, a barber and a janitor in a real estate office. Payton understood the power of Black business and creating jobs for Blacks. The Afro-American Realty Company developed a partnership of ten Blacks organized by Payton.

Wendell Campbell

(1971)

In 1971, Wendell Campbell was the co-founder and first president of the National Organization of Minority Architects (NOMA). NOMA was formed to promote minority-owned architectural firms. Campbell has served on the board of the Illinois Chapter of NOMA, the Cosmopolitan Chamber of Commerce, Mercy Hospital and Medical Center, the Black Ensemble Theater, the Chicago Chapter of the American Institute of Architects, the Chicago Architectural Assistance Center and the South Side YMCA. In 1966, he became the CEO of Wendell Campbell Associates, which since changed its name to Campbell Tiu Campbell to reflect the contributions of partners Domingo Tiu and Campbell's daughter, Susan.

Marie-Therese Métoyer

(1942)

Marie-Therese Métoyer was one of the most successful entrepreneurs in colonial America. She founded a prosperous community of free Blacks and Creoles in the Louisiana Province. Born August of 1942, Métoyer was a prominent médecine, planter, and businesswoman in Natchitoches Parish. She had been freed from slavery after a long liaison with Claude Métoyer that produced ten children. She and her descendants established the community of Creoles of color at Isle Brevelle, including what is believed to be the first church founded be free people of color, St. Augustine Parish Church, Natchez, Louisiana. The church is included on the Louisiana African-American Heritage Trail.

The New York Amsterdam News

(1909)

In 1909, *The New York Amsterdam News* was established by James H. Anderson. Begun in Harlem with only $10 in startup capital, the newspaper has continued to be one of the leading weekly African-American periodicals for over a century. Anderson originally sold copies of the newspaper for two cents each from his home. In 1935, the paper was sold to the Powell Savory Corporation, which was owned at the time by Dr. C. B. Powell. It was under Dr. Powell's leadership that *The New York Amsterdam News* began to flourish. *The New York Amsterdam News* is also the first African-American newspaper to have all of its departments unionized.

Charles C. Teamer, Sr.

(1983)

Charles C. Teamer, Sr. was the first African-American to be appointed to New Orleans' Board of Commissioners in 1983. In 1993, Teamer co-founded and served as Chairman of the Dryades Savings Bank. Teamer is a member of the board of supervisors for the University of Louisiana System and is on the board of administrators of Tulane University. Teamer is also the director of Entergy New Orleans, an electric and gas utility company and one of the two Fortune 500 companies located in New Orleans. He serves as President of the World Trade Center of New Orleans, a position he has held since 2000.

| 79 |

Clay Warren Coleman

(1867)

Clay Warren Coleman apprenticed under a plantation owner. Upon the completion of his training, he opened his own barbershop and pastry store in 1867. He was only 18. At 20, Coleman purchased a $600 piece of property. His entrepreneurial spirit propelled him to continue to open other small businesses and to purchase additional properties. In 1876, Coleman began lending money. He also became a real estate agent and broker. Coleman then built a cotton mill in 1901 that provided employment opportunities for Black workers. Ultimately, he became one of the wealthiest African-Americans in the South.

Courtesy of Black Enterprise Magazine.

Black Enterprise Magazine

(1970) Earl G. Graves, Sr. is the founder and publisher of *Black Enterprise* magazine and a noted authority on Black business development. In 2002, Fortune magazine named Graves one of the 50 most powerful and influential African-Americans in corporate America. He is chairman of Earl G. Graves Ltd., parent corporation of Earl G. Graves Publishing Co., the publisher of *Black Enterprise* magazine, a business-service publication founded in 1970 and targeted to Black professionals, executives, entrepreneurs, and policy makers in the public and private sectors. The magazine has a paid circulation of 525,000 with a readership of more than 3.9 million. Since 1997, the magazine has been a five-time recipient of the FOLIO: Editorial Excellence Award.

Trish Millines Dziko

(1996) Trish Millines Dziko is the co-founder and Executive Director of the Technology Access Foundation, a Seattle-based organization designed to provide science, technology, engineering, and mathematics skills to children of color. She became the full-time TAF Executive Director after leaving Microsoft in 1996. As one of the young Microsoft millionaires at 39, Dziko contributed significantly to establish TAF in 1996.

Addie L. Wyatt

(1953) Addie L. Wyatt, born March 18, 1924, became the first female board member of United Packinghouse Food & Alliance Workers Union. The organization is now referred to as the United Food and Commercial Workers International Union. Wyatt was elected Vice-President of Local 56 in 1953. As a union leader, she dedicated her career to speaking out against sexual and racial discrimination in the workplace. As recognition for her work, Wyatt (along with Congresswoman Barbara Jordan) was the first African-American woman to be named Person of the Year.

Philip Jenkins

(1955)

Philip Jenkins co-founded the first Black-owned and operated investment firm on Wall Street, Special Markets, Inc., and served as its president in 1955. This move also made Jenkins the first African-American president of an investment firm. Because of his reputation in the business world, the Black press dubbed Jenkins the "Wizard of Wall Street."

The Philadelphia Tribune

(1884)

The Philadelphia Tribune is the nation's oldest, and the Greater Philadelphia region's largest, daily newspaper serving the African-American community. Founded in 1884, the *Tribune's* circulation is just over 220,000 weekly. It is published five times a week in Philadelphia and available every day online. The *Tribune* has been recognized as the Best Newspaper in America by the National Newspaper Publishers Association.

Anthony Johnson

(1621)

Anthony Johnson, a Black man, arrived in Jamestown, Virginia in 1621 as an indentured servant. Under this construct – that indentured servants could work off their freedom after a period of time – Johnson was able to buy his freedom and accumulate 250 acres of property. Considered to be America's first Black entrepreneur, he was later able to hire his own Black and White servants and participate in the slave trade.

Elleanor Eldridge

(1785)

Elleanor Eldridge, born March 26, 1785, began washing clothes as a live-in servant. Eldridge made 25 cents a week doing laundry for a family at the age of 10. She also became skilled at spinning, arithmetic, and weaving, and was an accomplished weaver by age 14. Three years later, Eldridge began working as a dairy woman and became well-known for her premium-quality cheeses. When Eldridge was 19, her father died and she went to live with her sister in Adams, Massachusetts. While there, she and her brothers and sisters started a business of weaving, washing, and soap boiling. Money from that venture enabled Eldridge to buy land and build a house.

Courtesy of ESSENCE Magazine.

Essence Magazine

(1970)

In 1970, Essence Communications Inc. (ECI) launched *Essence* magazine, the ground-breaking publication created exclusively for African-American women in 1970. In 2000, Time, Inc. purchased 49 percent of the magazine, later buying the remaining 51 percent in a deal reported to be worth $170 million dollars. The company has expanded beyond the pages to generate brand extensions such as the Essence Music Festival, Women Who Are Shaping the World Leadership Summit, the Essence Book Club, Essence.com, and ventures in digital media (mobile, television, and Video on Demand) through Essence Studios. The publication has a monthly circulation of 1,050,000 and a readership of 8.5 million.

Sidney Wilhelm

(1970)

In Sidney Wilhelm's book, *Who Needs the Negro?*, published in 1970, Wilhelm states that as more technological advances are introduced into the workforce, the need for African-American labor decreases. Wilhelm continues his argument by asserting that as African-Americans receive more civil rights, they are considered more economically useless because of their perceived inability to keep up with a changing economy.

James P. Thomas

(1870)

By 1870, James P. Thomas had earned the reputation of being one of Missouri's wealthiest men. At his financial peak, the net worth of Thomas's estate was estimated at $250,000. Thomas was a successful barber with many influential White clients. He also managed his wife's 48 apartment units, which contributed significantly to his wealth. Thomas was the mulatto son of a prominent Nashville, Tennessee judge and a slave mother. Thomas's mother bought his freedom at age six. He began as a barber's apprentice before opening his own home-based shop. Because he was still considered a slave in Nashville, Thomas moved to Missouri.

Gertrude Pocte Geddes-Willis

(1880)

Gertrude Pocte Geddes-Willis, born March 18,1880, was one of the first American female funeral directors in New Orleans. In 1940, Mrs. Willis was founder and president of Gertrude Geddes Willis Life Insurance Company and Gertrude Geddes Willis Funeral Home. One of her special interests was youth development. Throughout her career, she gained the respect of both local and national business leaders.

The Negro Bankers Association

(1927)

In 1927, The Negro Bankers Association (NBA) was founded by Major R.R. Wright, then head of the Black-owned Philadelphia's Citizens and Southern Bank and Trust Company. In 1948, the NBA changed its name to the National Bankers Association to reflect the organization's plan for expansion. The NBA is an advocacy group for minority- and women-owned banks. It advises its members about legislative and regulatory matters concerning the banking industry and the communities their banks serve. Initially, the NBA included 14 Black-owned banks.

Third World Press (TWP)

(1967)

Third World Press (TWP) is one of the nation's oldest independent publishers of Black literature. In 1967, Haki R. Madhubuti laid the foundation for TWP with the help of Johari Amini and Carolyn Rodgers. *The Covenant with Black America* edited by Tavis Smiley is the first book published by a Black-owned company ever to appear on the New York Times' nonfiction best-seller list.

| 83 |

Charles Avant

(1967)

Charles Avant, former night club and artist manager, founded Venture Records, Inc., in 1967 to become an outlet for MGM Records' soul acts. This became the first joint venture between an African-American artist and a major record company. Under Avant Garde Broadcasting, Avant bought the first African-American--owned FM radio station in metropolitan Los Angeles.

Library of Congress Prints and Photographs Division, Washington, DC.

Parren J. Mitchell

(1971)

The first Black representative from Maryland, Parren J. Mitchell, was sworn in as a member of the Ninety-second Congress in 1971. At the beginning of the Ninety-seventh Congress in 1981, Mitchell was Chairman of the Committee on Small Business. Mitchell championed minority-owned businesses and small firms, and one of his greatest accomplishments was an amendment to a $4-billion public works program requiring state and local governments applying for federal contracts to reserve 10 percent for minority-owned companies. Mitchell's prime focus was on improving minority residents' welfare in Baltimore as well as other urban centers.

Edward Boyd

(1947)

In 1947, Edward Boyd was appointed by Pepsi-Cola to lead an all-Black sales force to promote Pepsi to the African-American community. Boyd's success story gained national attention with the release of the book *The Real Pepsi Challenge: The Inspirational Story of Breaking the Color Barrier in American Business.*

The Nation of Islam's (NOI)
Three-Year Economic Savings Program

(1964)

The Nation of Islam's (NOI) Three-Year Economic Savings Program was established by the Honorable Elijah Muhammad in 1964. This program called for Black people to pool their resources by contributing $10 a month to help fight poverty, unemployment, abominable housing, and hunger in the Black communities of America. The Honorable Minister Louis Farrakhan re-established this program in October 1991 to address the economic problems facing Black Americans today. In December 1994, the NOI purchased some farmland located in Bronwood, Georgia with contributions from the Three-Year Economic Savings Program. The farm, which is called Muhammad Farms, was once part of a 4,500-acre farm owned by the Nation of Islam until the 1970s.

Rosewood, Florida

(1995)

In 1995, Rosewood, Florida was the first African-American community to seek and receive reparations for the destruction of property and murder of its citizens. Nine of the 21 known survivors were paid $150,000 each by the State of Florida after local Whites destroyed the entire Black community on New Year's Day 1923.

Cody Bryant

(1905)

Jasper County, Georgia was home to Cody Bryant, heralded as "one of the richest Colored farmers in the U.S." Bryant owned a 1,650-acre estate and employed twenty African-American workers to help him manage the property. In 1905, Bryant's harvest yielded 415 bales of cotton, 4,000 bushels of corn, 1,200 bushels of wheat, 900 bushels of oats, 1,000 bushels of potatoes, 475 bushels of peas, and 6,335 gallons of syrup. Bryant was said to be worth $200,000 in William Ferris's book, *The African Abroad: or his Evolution in Western Civilization.*

Willi Smith

(1967)

Willi Smith, one of the most successful African-American fashion designers in history, began his design career in 1967. By 1969, Smith had achieved success with the sportswear company, Digits. Smith went on to create WilliWear, which achieved $25 million a year in its heyday. Before long the streetwise and sassy WilliWear designs caught the public's attention in a big way, and other designers soon copied the style. Willi Smith entered popular culture when he designed Mary Jane's wedding dress for the *Spider-Man* comic book and comic strip in 1987. Additionally, he designed clothing for Spike Lee's -film "School Daze" in 1987.

Ulysses Bridgeman, Jr.

(1987)

Upon retiring from the NBA in 1987, Ulysses Bridgeman, Jr. bought five Wendy's franchises to generate income while he planned his next career. Today, he controls a sprawling dining empire with 161 Wendy's and 118 Chili's locations. Last year, sales of his Manna Inc. holding company were $530 million.

© Cathy Hughes.

Radio One, Inc.

(1980)

Founded in 1980, Radio One, Inc. is one of the nation's largest radio broadcasting companies and the largest such company primarily targeting African-American and urban listeners. The company is led by Chairperson and Founder Catherine L. Hughes, and her son, Alfred C. Liggins, III. Radio One, headquartered in Lanham, MD, owns and/or operates over 50 radio stations located in over 15 urban markets in the United States. Additionally, Radio One also holds interests in TV One, LLC, a cable/satellite network with programming targeted primarily to African-Americans. Radio One's initial public offering of common stock was on May 5, 1999.

John W. Rogers

(1983)

In 1983, John W. Rogers started Ariel Capital Management, Inc. At the time, Rogers' Black-owned business had only one major account: $100,000 worth of Howard University's endowment fund. Within six months, Rogers raised an additional $190,000 in investment funds. As of 2004, Ariel managed about $17.4 billion in investments, and it currently manages up to $5.4 billion today under the name Ariel Investments.

| 86 |

Lt. Colonel Allen Allensworth

(1908)

In 1908, Lt. Colonel Allen Allensworth founded the township of Allensworth, California which served as a business center for African-Americans. He was inspired with the idea of establishing a self-sufficient, all-Black California community where African-Americans could live their lives free of the racial discrimination that pervaded post-Reconstruction, turn-of-the-century America. Allensworth became a haven for Blacks seeking to live free of racial discrimination. Additionally, as a soldier in the U.S. Army, Allensworth ascended to the rank of Lt. Colonel, the highest rank for an African-American at the time.

Quintin Primo, III

(1992)

Quintin Primo, III founded Capri Capital in 1992 with childhood friend Daryl Carter and achieved initial success by extending mezzanine loans to small borrowers that larger firms neglected to serve. Capri's portfolio includes a significant amount of apartment complexes. The firm's assets under management have swelled to $4.3 billion.

North Carolina A&T Four

(1960)

Ezell A. Blair, Jr., David Richmond, Joseph McNeil, and Franklin McCain, students at North Carolina's A&T University, became known as the NC A&T Four, or the Greensboro Four, when they sat in at a segregated Woolworth's lunch counter in downtown Greensboro, North Carolina on February 1, 1960. The sit-ins were planned by the Bennett College chapter of the NAACP, advised by John Hatchett, and had the full support and participation of Bennett students. Within 2 months the sit-in movement had spread to 54 cities and 9 states.

Just Us Books

(1988)

Founded in 1988 by the husband-and-wife team of Wade and Cheryl Hudson, Just Us Books is a leading publisher of books for young people that focus on African-American history, culture, and experiences. Combining their experience in marketing and graphic design, the couple developed a number of manuscripts using Afro-centric themes and images.

R. Donahue Peebles

(1988)

R. Donahue Peebles is chairman and chief executive officer of The Peebles Corporation, the country's largest African-American real estate development company with a $4-billion development portfolio. Founded in 1988, the company's portfolio consists of luxury hotel, high-rise residential, and Class A commercial properties and developments which are located in Washington, DC, San Francisco, Las Vegas, and Miami Beach.

Courtesy by Lonnie Major.

Robert Johnson

(1991)

In 1991, Black Entertainment Television (BET) became the first Black-owned company traded on the New York Stock Exchange. Based in Washington, DC, BET was launched in 1980 with an investment of $15,000. By 1993, it was a $61-million media enterprise. In 2001, BET was sold to Viacom for $3 billion. In 2007, BET expanded its influence through the creation of related cable networks Centric, BET Gospel, and BET Hip-Hop. Its former owner, Robert L. Johnson, became the first Black billionaire, listed at #172 on the Forbes list of richest Americans.

Omar Wasow

(1999)

Omar Wasow co-founded BlackPlanet.com, a social networking site targeted especially for the African-American community. Under Omar's leadership, BlackPlanet.com became the leading site for African-Americans, reaching over three million people a month. BlackPlanet.com was launched in September 1999, and in December 2007 it was the 4th highest-trafficked social-networking site.

The Freedman's Savings and Trust Company

(1864)

The Freedman's Savings and Trust Company began as a savings bank for African-American soldiers that had no safe place to deposit their money. Freedmen's Savings and Trust Company was launched in 1864 to eliminate individual bank mismanagement and bring all of the Black deposits under central control in a single large institution. In 1868, the bank's headquarters was moved to Washington, DC, where Black staffers were trained to take over its operations. At its peak, the bank operated 37 branches in 17 states and the District of Columbia, making it one of the first multi-state banks in the nation.

The Woman's Convention

(1900)

The Woman's Convention, Auxiliary to the National Baptist Convention, was organized in September 1900 primarily to raise money. The money provided food, clothing, housing, and educational opportunities for poor people in the United States and around the world. The work of the Convention was directed by an Executive Committee of twelve members.

Jesse B. Blayton

(1949)

In 1949, Jesse B. Blayton, a bank president and professor at Atlanta University, purchased the radio station WERD for $50,000. It was the first radio station in America owned by an African-American. The station's announcers were African-American and its format featured music and other programming of interest to the local African-American community. Blayton was also Georgia's first African-American Certified Public Accountant (CPA) and the fourth in the United States. Through his work as a professor and the encouragement he gave to his students, Blayton was known as the "Dean of Negro Accountants."

Jean Baptiste Pointe du Sable

(1745)

Born in Haiti in 1745, Jean Baptiste Pointe du Sable established the first permanent settlement in present-day Chicago. He set up a trading post supplying customers with wheat, flour, meats, and furs for cash and durable goods. Du Sable had established a good reputation with trading relations as far away as Green Bay, Detroit, and Canada.

Sylvia Woods

(1962)

Sylvia Woods is the founder and owner of Sylvia's Restaurant, located in Harlem since 1962. She became a waitress at a luncheonette and later bought the business after her mother mortgaged her farm for the loan. Today, the family-owned enterprise consists of Sylvia's Restaurant in Harlem, a full-service catering hall, Sylvia's Catering Corp., a nationwide line of Sylvia's Food Products, and two cookbooks.

Courtesy of Operation HOPE

Operation HOPE

(1992)

John Hope Bryant is a best-selling author and the founder, chairman, and chief executive officer of Operation HOPE, Inc., the financial literacy empowerment nonprofit. Bryant launched Operation HOPE, Inc. following the civil unrest of April 1992 in Los Angeles. In 18 years, the nonprofit has provided financial literacy and economic empowerment services to more than 1.2 million people, raised more than $500 million, and helped to restructure more than $360 million in sub-prime mortgages from the private sector, for a total of approximately $900 million in economic activity for the disenfranchised. Operation HOPE proclaims itself to be an organization "Leading a Global Silver Rights Movement in the 21st Century through economic empowerment."

Mutual Benefit Societies

(1800s)

Mutual Benefit Societies were to provide a pool of resources from which members and their families could draw benefits otherwise denied to African-Americans, such as burial insurance and financial aid in times of sickness. During the 1800's, the societies also provided financial assistance to widows, orphans, and the disabled. Their membership constituted a diverse segment of the African-American community while their leaders were mainly merchants and ministers.

William Mays

(1980)

William Mays is President and CEO of Mays Chemical Company, one of the nation's largest chemical distribution companies. Founded in 1980, the company is an integrated chemical distributor, and a source for chemicals, raw materials, cleaning and sanitation systems, and chemical management expertise. Mays owns *The Indianapolis Recorder,* the fourth-oldest African-American newspaper in the United States.

Dave Bing

(1981)

Upon retiring from the NBA, Dave Bing founded Bing Steel in Detroit, which became a $61 million enterprise within a decade of its 1981 inception. The Bing Group bought out a metal stamping firm and added a construction company and grossed sales of more than $135 million. This made Bing's group *Black Enterprise's* 32nd top industrial/service company in 2006, and in 2009, Bing was elected mayor of Detroit, MI.

Sara Knight Preddy

(1951)

Sara Knight Preddy is the first woman of color to own both a non-restrictive gaming license and a major hotel in the United States. In 1951, she borrowed $600 from her father to purchase Hawthorne's, the one club for Blacks and renamed it the Tonga Club. She hosted the likes of Sammy Davis, Jr., Pearl Bailey, Nat King Cole, Eartha Kitt, and Joe Louis. Sara owned and operated well-known gaming establishments such as the Playhouse Lounge and The People's Choice, and numerous other businesses including a dry cleaner and a clothing store. Sara reopened the Moulin Rouge, which was the first racially integrated hotel-casino in Las Vegas.

Percy Miller

(1998)

As founder and CEO of No Limit Entertainment, Percy Miller at one time presided over a business empire that included No Limit Records, Bout It Inc., No Limit Clothing, No Limit Films, No Limit Sports Management, PM. Properties, and Advantage Travel. Miller ranked 10th on *Forbes* magazine's 1998 list of America's 40 highest-paid entertainers.

| 91 |

William Reuben Pettiford

(1890)

In 1890, Alabama minister William Reuben Pettiford founded and became President of the Alabama Penny Savings and Loan Company, Alabama's first Black-owned and operated bank. Under Pettiford's guidance, the company survived one financial depression in 1893 and another in 1913. Due to its success, Penny Savings eventually opened branches in Selma, Anniston, and Montgomery. On July 15, 1902, the deposits were $78,124.21, and by October 1911, they had reached $421,596.51. Much of the bank's success resulted from Pettiford's and the directors' emphasis on homeownership. By the time of Pettiford's death, Alabama Penny Savings and Loan was regarded as one of the best-managed banks in the country.

Courtesy of Andrea Harris, North Carolina Institute of Minority Economic Development.

Parrish Street
(1900) Known nationally as "Black Wall Street," Parrish Street bordered the Hayti area of Durham, North Carolina, the primary residential area for African-Americans. During the 1900's some noteworthy businesses included the North Carolina Mutual Life Insurance Company and the Mechanics and Farmers Bank. Black leaders W.E.B. DuBois and Booker T. Washington felt that Parrish Street exemplified the Black middle class on a national level.

Archie Givens, Sr.
(1919) Archie Givens, Sr., born in 1919, was a trailblazer, a mentor, a visionary, and an entrepreneur who inspired many others to follow his pursuit of excellence. As a successful businessman, he established two major enterprises in Minneapolis, Minnesota, The Willows Convalescent Centers, a nursing home company, and Rainbow Development Company, a real estate company.

Alonzo F. Herndon
(1878) Alonzo F. Herndon had only one year of formal education, but learned barbering in Jonesboro, Georgia, where in 1878 he opened his first barbershop. Herndon moved to Atlanta in 1882 and opened three barbershops. One of the barbershops, the thirty-three chair Crystal Palace at 66 Peachtree Street, was considered the most elegant in the country. He invested his barbering income in real estate, becoming by the early 1900's the largest Black property owner in Atlanta. His most significant business venture was launched in 1905, when he acquired what would become Atlanta Life Insurance Company, today the largest Black-owned stockholder insurance company in America.

Mary Ann Prout

(1867)

Mary Ann Prout founded the Independent Order of St. Luke in 1867. St. Luke was a Baltimore-based women's mutual insurance society that provided care for the sick and burial of the dead. The mutual society was one of many dedicated to supporting the social and financial advancement of the Black community.

WGPR-TV

(1975)

William V. Banks and George White are founders of the first African-American--owned and operated television station in the United States, WGPR-TV in Detroit, Michigan. First airing on September 29, 1975, WGPR-TV was the first station to have African-Americans behind the cameras and microphones as well as making programming decisions and creating schedules. Hundreds of minorities trained at WGPR went on to become successful on-air personalities, anchors, and journalists for networks such as ABC, NBC, CBS, and their affiliates.

Russell Simmons

(2005)

Russell Simmons founded Rush Communications, the 11th largest Black-owned business in the nation. Rush Communications boasted $360 million in revenue in 2005. Simmons' net worth is estimated between $325–500 million. Additionally, Simmons is co-founder of the pioneering hip-hop label Def-Jam Records.

Sheila Johnson

(2008)

Sheila C. Johnson, a successful entrepreneur and impassioned philanthropist, is CEO of Salamander Hospitality, LLC, overseeing a growing portfolio of luxury properties such as the Woodlands Resort & Inn in Summerville, South Carolina. Johnson is president and managing partner of the WNBA's Washington Mystics. She has also been very influential in the entertainment industry as a founding partner of Black Entertainment Television (BET) and, most recently, as a film producer. Her film *A Powerful Noise* premiered at the 2008 Tribeca Film Festival in New York, and on March 5, 2009 premiered in more than 450 theatres throughout the country.

Rainbow Push Wall Street Project

(1996) When Operation PUSH and the National Rainbow Coalition merged, their founder, Reverend Jesse Jackson, created a formidable force for social justice. Jackson joined with prominent business leaders to launch the Wall Street Project to promote minority-owned businesses. The Wall Street Project's mission is to encourage private and public businesses to improve hiring and promoting practices for minorities, name more minorities to corporate boards, allocate more business to minority-owned companies, and increase financial dealings between minority businesses. Some of the Project's accomplishments include its yearly career expo, as well as the Media and Telecommunications Project (MTP) in Washington, DC and the Peachtree Street Project in Atlanta, GA.

William Latham

(1917) In 1917, Attorney William Latham founded Underwriters Insurance Company in Chicago, becoming the first Black insurance company north of the Mason-Dixon Line. The insurance company handled many of the riot cases that grew out of the Chicago Race Riots of 1919.

Oscar Micheaux

(1905) Oscar Micheaux founded the Micheaux Film and Book Company, one of the few Black-owned film companies to survive the transition into the sound era. In 1905, Micheaux acquired 160-acres in South Dakota. Micheaux published his first novel in 1913, *The Conquest of a Negro Pioneer,* which he self-published and distributed, selling it door-to-door to small businessmen and other homesteaders. Already a successful businessman and author, Micheaux's first film was "Homesteader" in 1919, based on his novel. He went on to produce 27 other films. He is the first African-American independent film director and producer.

The National Black MBA Association

(1972)

The National Black MBA Association is a network of business professionals with a commitment to education, career development, and promoting the economic wealth of the African-American community. Founded in 1972, the organization has 44 professional chapters nationwide and 15 Collegiate Chapters with membership across the country and around the world.

Elizabeth Denison Forth

(1825)

Elizabeth Denison Forth was born a slave. However, she purchased four lots that totaled 48.5 acres in Pontiac, Michigan in 1825. Having worked as a domestic for wealthy homeowners, Forth learned from them how to invest and acquire land. With her wages as a domestic worker, she purchased stock in the steamboat Michigan and twenty shares of the Farmers and Mechanics Bank. Forth contributed to Saint James Protestant Episcopal Church. Her contributions provided a new chapel where parishioners of diverse ethnic and social classes could worship together.

Thomy Lafon

(1868)

In 1868, Thomy Lafon began to build his fortune from real estate and businesses. The wealth he had amassed by 1870 made him one of the wealthiest African-Americans in the nation. Lafon is mostly known for his large donations to such causes as the American Anti-Slavery Society, the Underground Railroad, and the Louisiana Association for the Benefit of Colored Orphans.

| 95 |

Dr. James Durham

(1762)

Dr. James Durham, born into slavery in 1762, buys his freedom and begins his own medical practice in New Orleans, becoming the first African-American doctor in the United States. As a youngster he worked for doctors who taught him how to read and write, mix medicines, and work with patients. Durham had a flourishing medical practice in New Orleans until 1801 when the city restricted his practice because he did not have a formal medical degree.

Courtesy of Industrial Bank.

Industrial Bank

(1934) Jesse H. Mitchell and nine other businessmen from Washington, DC founded Industrial Bank in 1934. Today, Industrial Bank is the largest minority-owned commercial bank in the nation's capital. Industrial Bank has grown from six employees and $192,000 in assets into an institution with over 150 employees and more than $333 million in assets, making it the fourth largest minority-owned financial institution in the country. Industrial Bank works with the community through public/private partner-ships, banking education seminars, and sponsorships.

B. (Barbara) Smith

(1986) B. (Barbara) Smith began her career as a fashion model. In 1986, Smith opened the first of three successful B. Smith Restaurants. The B. Smith with Style Home Collection is the first line from an African-American woman to be sold at nationwide retailers. Smith has created and produced cable television shows focusing on the B. Smith brand.

Emergency Land Fund (ELF)

(1972) Emergency Land Fund (ELF) was formally organized in 1972 with the mission to create United States policies that supported and protected Black land ownership, especially among Black farmers. ELF was a direct response to news and government reports of rapid loss of land owned by African-Americans and the lack of resources or support to maintain farms. In 1981, with a grant from the United States Department of Agriculture, the ELF conducted research on heir property in the rural south. The study is known as *The Impact of Heir Property on Black Rural Land Tenure in the Southeastern United States.*

Willie E. Gary

(1947)

Willie E. Gary is one of America's most well-known attorneys. Born in 1947 in Eastman, GA, Gary has won some of the largest jury awards and settlements in United States history, including more than 150 cases valued in excess of $1 million each. Forbes magazine has listed him as one of the Top 50 Attorneys in the United States.

Archie Alexander

(1888)

Archie Alexander, born May 14, 1888, was an African-American designer and construction engineer, responsible for the construction of Whitehurst Freeway, the Tidal Basin and an extension to the Baltimore-Washington Parkway. In 1929, Alexander and his White former classmate, Maurice A. Repass, partnered to form Alexander & Repass, an engineering firm. In 1949, Ebony magazine called their firm the "nation's most successful interracial business." Alexander was the only Black student at the College of Engineering in Iowa City. He wasn't appointed to any of the engineering positions in which he applied upon graduation, in 1912. As a manual laborer for the Marsh Engineering Company, Alexander proved his skill within a couple years and was in charge of the Marsh Engineering Company bridge building program.

Richard R. Wright, Sr.

(1855)

Richard R. Wright, Sr., born in 1855, worked as a school founder, educator, newspaper publisher, entrepreneur, political organizer, banker, and scholar. Wright opened the first trust company organized by African-Americans, Citizens and Southern Bank and Trust Company. In 1927, Wright and C.C. Spaulding joined with 70 other black bankers to form the National Association of Negro Bankers.

| 97 |

Liberty Bank

(1972)

Founded in 1972, Liberty Bank's primary focus is bringing financial services to the underserved in the New Orleans community. One of the five largest African-American--owned financial institutions, Liberty is a corporate partner of Fortune 500 companies, and a major supplier of financial services to government agencies. Within the last decade, Liberty has grown from $50 million to $340 million in total assets.

Courtesy of Ira Block.

Reginald F. Lewis

(1983)

Reginald F. Lewis opened the first African-American law firm on Wall Street. He focused on corporate law and assisted many minority-owned businesses in securing capital using Minority Enterprise Small Business Investment Companies. In 1983, Lewis established the TLC Group L.P. His first major deal involved the $22.5-million leveraged buyout of the McCall Pattern Company. He later sold it for $90 million. In October 1987, Lewis purchased the international division of Beatrice Foods which became known as TLC Beatrice International. At $985 million, this deal was the largest leveraged buyout of overseas assets by an American company at the time. As Chairman and CEO, Lewis led a company which had sales of over $1.6 billion annually.

Nannie Helen Burroughs

(1909)

Nannie Helen Burroughs was inspired to open her own school after being denied a teaching job due to the color of her skin. On October 19, 1909 in the Lincoln Heights section of Washington, DC, she opened the National Training School for Women and Girls. Vocational training classes were taught in domestic science, social work, home nursing, clerical work, printing, dress making, beauty culture, and agriculture.

(1927) ## The National Bankers Association

The National Bankers Association was founded in 1927 to serve as an advocate for the nation's minority- and women-owned banks. Richard R. Wright, Jr., a Philadelphia banker, and C.C. Spaulding, a North Carolina insurance business-man, called bankers together to create the organization. This first formal national organization of minority banks' initial membership totaled 14 African-American banks.

Operation Fair Share Program

(1981)

In 1981, the NAACP initiated the Operation Fair Share Program in an effort to increase employment and strengthen minority entrepreneurship. Administered by the NAACP Development Department, the goal was to build a working relationship with private sector firms that would encourage more job opportunities and other economic benefits for Blacks.

Scott Bond

(1874)

In 1874, Scott Bond, at the age of twenty-two, began renting a portion of the 2,200 acre Allen farm in Arkansas. Bond paid in cash for his rental property and managed the property for eleven years. He later bought a second farm of 300 acres while still maintaining his property portion of the Allen farm. Bond's business acumen was attributed to several more purchases including farms, four town lot purchases, five cotton gin plants and a sawmill.

Shawn Carter (JAY-Z)

(1969)

Born December 4, 1969, Shawn Carter is one of the most financially successful hip-hop artists and entrepreneurs in America. Better known as JAY-Z, he is founder and chairman of Rocawear, co-owner of the New Jersey Nets, 40/40 clubs, Translation Advertising, and Carol's Daughter. JAY-Z is past President and CEO of Def Jam Recordings. JAY-Z released "Blueprint 3," his 11th #1 album -- the most by any solo artist.

| 99 |

Auburn Avenue

(1956)

In 1956, *Forbes* magazine dubbed Atlanta, Georgia's Auburn Avenue the "richest Negro street in the world." In a South that remained segregated, Auburn, also called "Sweet Auburn," was home to Atlanta's burgeoning African-American middle-class from 1893 until the 1930's. Auburn Avenue was also the home of the Atlanta Life Insurance Company, the *Atlanta Daily Word* (the first Black-owned daily newspaper), and the Royal Peacock Club (an elegant club in which many popular African-American music artists performed).

Courtesy of The Kennedy Center.

Bill and Camille Cosby

(1988) Bill and Camille Cosby delivered a gift to Spelman College of $20 million in 1988, the largest single donation to a historically Black college or university, as well as the largest single charitable contribution given by African-Americans at the time. Bill Cosby has dazzled generations of fans with his comedy routines, many captured in his iconic albums, in best-selling books such as *Fatherhood,* and on the groundbreaking TV series "The Cosby Show." His wife, producer and educator Dr. Camille O. Cosby, co-produced the Broadway run of Having Our Say which earned three Tony nominations and won the 1999 Peabody Award for the highly rated, made-for-television film of *Having Our Say* on CBS (April 1999).

Jesse Russell

(1948) In 1948, Jesse Russell is currently Chairman and CEO of incNETWORKS. He is the recognized father of digital cellular technology and is responsible for many of the innovations found in the world's wireless infrastructure. He holds over 75 patents in digital cellular technologies, dual-mode digital cellular phones, and digital software radio associated with this billion-dollar industry.

Associated Negro Press

(1919) In 1919, Claude Barnett, influenced by Booker T. Washington's philosophy of self-help and service to the race, established the first national news service for African-Americans. The Associated Negro Press (ANP) carried detailed coverage of news within the Black community. It also provided news stories, opinion columns, feature stories, and book and movie reviews to Black newspapers across the country. The Associated Negro Press served over 200 subscribers. Following World War II, its membership also included over 100 Black newspapers.

Sarah E. Goode

(1885)

Sarah E. Goode was the first African-American woman to be granted a patent by the U.S. Patent and Trademark Office for her invention, the cabinet bed, on July 14, 1885. As owner of a furniture store, she noted that city apartment dwellers often had little space for beds. She conceived the design of what we know today as the "hide-away" bed.

David Ruggles

(1810)

Abolitionist David Ruggles, born in 1810, was a man of many firsts. Ruggles' holdings included the first African-American--owned bookstore, and he held the distinction of publishing the *Mirror of Liberty*, the first periodical published by an African-American. The later accomplishment also established Ruggles as one of the first African-American journalists. Ruggles also opened a grocery store in 1827 before opening the bookstore in 1834. He mostly sold publications and prints that promoted the abolition of slavery and opposed the American Colonization Society which favored Black settlements in Liberia.

Center for the Study of Black Business, History, Entrepreneurship and Technology

(2002)

The Center for the Study of Black Business, History, Entrepreneurship and Technology was founded at the University of Texas at Austin in 2002 by Professor Juliet E. K. Walker. The Center provides a comprehensive study of all aspects of Black business from various disciplines in the liberal arts and within the context of the impact of racial capitalism on Black business activity.

Air Atlanta

(1984)

Air Atlanta was founded in February of 1984 by Michael Hollis. He received initial backing from the National Alliance of Federal and Postal Employees, a Black union whose pension fund committed $500,000 to invest as venture capital. Air Atlanta had nearly $90 million in start-up funding by the time it took to the skies.

Courtesy of Alexis Herman.

Alexis Herman

(1997)

Alexis Herman was appointed Secretary of Labor by President Clinton in 1997 during his second term. Herman also served as advisor to President Carter and Labor Secretary Ray Marshall. She advised on matters of economic and social concern to women in the workplace. She also directed the department's program for developing businesses. At 29, Herman was the youngest director to serve in the Women's Bureau. Previously, Herman developed a program for Atlanta's Southern Regional Council that recruited and trained African-Americans, primarily women, for white-collar employment opportunities in the construction business.

Juanita Britton

(1990)

The first African-American Kwanzaa and Christmas Bazaar in Washington, DC was held in 1990 and organized by Juanita Britton. The Bazaar was a showcase for many Black artisans to show their work. Because of Britton's promotion and marketing skills, the Bazaar is a yearly and lucrative success. Later, she expanded her business by becoming the first African-American to own a Brooks Brothers franchise. She owns two locations in the DC-area airports and five CNBC stores and two PGA Golf Stores.

Eddie C. Brown

(1983)

Eddie C. Brown is founder and President of Brown Capital Management in Baltimore, one of the country's oldest African-American--owned investment management firms, which he started in 1983. He served as Vice President and portfolio manager for T. Rowe Price Associates prior to starting his own firm. Brown was voted Ernst & Young's Entrepreneur of the Year in the financial services category for the State of Maryland in 2003. In April of the following year, he was inducted into the Maryland Chamber of Commerce Business Hall of Fame. In 2002, Brown and his family had announced the creation of the Turning the Corner Achievement Program (TCAP), an educational initiative for African-American middle school students in Baltimore.

Carol's Daughter

(1999)

Brooklyn native Lisa Price began experimenting with fragrance, essential oils and natural moisturizers to make gifts for her family and friends. The demand for her unparalleled hair and body care products led to a highly successful mail-order and web-based business. In 1999, Carol's Daughter opened its first boutique in the cozy confines of Brooklyn's Fort Greene neighborhood. The store's success lead to appearances of Carol's Daughter products on top national television shows, including The Today Show, The View and The Oprah Winfrey Show. In 2005, Carol's Daughter introduced new product packaging, an updated website, announced exciting celebrity investors and a highly anticipated Harlem flagship store in New York City.

Walter Cohen

(1910)

In 1910, Walter Cohen and other investors founded the People's Benevolent Life Insurance Company. In 1942, the insurance company had assets of $300,000 and total insurance of $5,874,946. By 1961, the company had grown substantially, amassing assets worth $2.8 million. Cohen also established the People's Drug Store in New Orleans, which later expanded to a second store. Cohen was one of the few African-Americans to be a politician during the post-Reconstruction era; he served as Customs Inspector, Registrar of the U.S. Land Office, and Comptroller of Customs.

American League of Colored Laborers

| 103 |

(1850)

In July 1850, African-American skilled workers in New York City organized the American League of Colored Laborers. The League sought to encourage unity among African-American mechanics and other trades people and help them establish their own businesses. It also promoted the training of young African-Americans in agriculture, commerce, and industrial crafts.

National Black United Fund

(1972)

Founded in 1972, the mission of the National Black United Fund is to build a viable philanthropic institution for Black American opportunity, growth, and change. Using philanthropic resources to meet vital needs in Black communities, the Fund also mobilizes those resources as venture capital to leverage social and economic change.

Courtesy of www.officialkwanzaawebsite.org

Kwanzaa

(1966) 1966 witnessed the first celebration of Kwanzaa. Kwanzaa is an African-American cultural holiday that was imagined and created by Dr. Maulana Ron Karenga. The holiday is customarily celebrated from December 26th through January 1st, and is focused on Nguzo Saba, the Seven Principles. The Seven Principles are Unity, Self-Determination, Collective Work and Responsibility, Cooperative Economics, Purpose, Creativity, and Faith. The term Kwanzaa is a derivation of the Swahili phrase matunda ya kwanza, or the first fruits of the harvest. On December 29th, ujamaa-- or Cooperative Economics--is celebrated.

The Sullivan Principle

(1971) Rev. Leon Sullivan joined the Board of Directors at General Motors in 1971 and used his corporate foothold to develop ideal terms for corporate America to do business in South African. The Sullivan Principles outlined standards for fair pay and treatment, for shared governance, and for the eventual dismantling of apartheid. Because General Motors was the largest employer of Blacks in South Africa, and because they adhered to the Sullivan Principles, many other employers agreed to implement the principles in their workplaces. While more gradual than the divestment movement, which suggested boycotts of companies doing business with South Africa, the Sullivan Principles were partly responsible for the dismantling of apartheid.

The Great Depression

(1929) In 1929, The Great Depression commenced with the crash of the New York Stock Market. Unemployment for African-Americans exceeded 50 percent by 1932. The high numbers of unemployed African-Americans were greatly impacted by racism. The notion that if Whites could not find work then Blacks should not be given work galvanized many White workers' attempts to keep Blacks unemployed. Blacks also fell victim to the practice of "last hired, first fired." In the South, African-Americans were already becoming more displaced due to new technology and falling crop prices; as a result, they moved toward northern, western, and southern cities to look for jobs in an already hostile environment.

Wilberforce University

(1856)

Wilberforce University was founded in 1856 with ties to the Methodist Episcopal Church in Wilberforce, Ohio, but closed its doors six years later due to a lowered enrollment and poor financial support because of the Civil War. The African Methodist Episcopal Church (AME) bought and reopened the institution in 1861, making it the first university owned and operated by African-Americans.

William C. Nell

(1863)

William C. Nell was the first African-American federal employee. In 1863, he was employed as a postal clerk in the Boston post office. As a young man, Nell was greatly inspired by *The Liberator,* an anti-slavery newspaper created by abolitionist William Lloyd Garrison in 1831. Born in 1816, Nell was a devoted abolitionist. He worked with Garrison and *The Liberator,* running the magazine's employment bureau for free African-Americans and fugitive slaves. Nell also lobbied tirelessly for the integration of schools in the state of Massachusetts. He was eventually successful and Massachusetts state schools were integrated in 1855.

National Association of Black Accountants

(1969)

In December 1969, nine African-Americans met in New York City to discuss the challenges and limited opportunities faced in the accounting profession. This meeting resulted in the formulation of the National Association of Black Accountants. In that year, there were only 136 African-American Certified Public Accountants (CPAs) in the United States. **Today there are over 200,000 African-Americans participating in the field of accounting, of which over 5,000 are CPAs.**

Maryland Freedom Union

(1966)

In 1966, the Maryland Freedom Union (MFU) was formed by 20 Black women who worked as nurses' aides, housekeepers, and kitchen staff for the Lincoln Nursing Home in Baltimore, Maryland. The women walked off their jobs, fed up with working up to 72 hours per work week for as little as 25 cents per hour. The union was also successful in negotiating with Silverman's Department Store chain from which it won a recognition agreement.

APPENDIX

INDEX

INDEX_____

INDEX_____

BIBLIOGRAPHY

This is not an exhaustive list of the sources referenced to develop this compendium of Black Economic History Facts. For the interested reader, however, it offers a place to start in order to learn more about the awesome history of African-Americans in the U.S. economy.

America, R. F. (1993). *Paying the Social Debt: What White America Owes Black America.* Westport, Conn.: Praeger.

Bell, Gregory (2001). *In the Black: A History of African-Americans* on Wall Street. New York: Wiley.

Bennett, Lerone (1988). *Before the Mayflower: A History of Black America,* New York: Penguin Books.

Berry, Mary Frances and Blassingame, John W. (1982). *Long Memory: The Black Experience in America,* Chapter 6, "The Economics of Hope and Despair," New York: Oxford University Press.

Bocian, Debbie Gruenstein, et al., *Foreclosures by Race and Ethnicity: The Demographics of a Crisis,* Center for Responsible Lending, June, 2010.

Bundles, A'lelia (2001). *On Her Own Ground: The Life and Times of Madame C.J. Walker.* New York: Washington Square Press.

Bureau of Labor Statistics, The Employment Situation, June 2010, USDL-10-0886.

Butler, John Sibley (2005). *Entrepreneurship and Self-Help Among African Americans: A Reconsideration of Race and Economics.* State University of New York Press.

Conley, D. (1999). *Being Black and Living in the Red: Race, Wealth, And Social Policy in America.* Berkeley: University of California Press.

Cruse, Harold (1967). *The Crisis of the Negro Intellectual.* New York: Morrow.

Franklin, John Hope (1987). *From Slavery to Freedom: A History of Negro Americans.* New York: Alfred A. Knopf.

Franklin, John Hope (1994). *Reconstruction after the Civil War.* Chicago: University of Chicago Press.

Franklin, John Hope (2005). *Mirror to America: The Autobiography of John Hope Franklin.* New York: Farrar, Straus and Giroux.

Gibson, D. Parke (1969). *The $30 Billion Negro.* New York: Macmillan.

Gibson, D. Parke (1978). *$70 Billion in the Black: America's Black Consumers.* New York: Macmillan.

Githinji, M. wa and Mason, P. L. (2008). Excavating for Economics in Africana Studies. *Journal of Black Studies.*

Gordon Nembhard, J. and Chiteji, N. (eds.) (2006). *Wealth Accumulation and Communities of Color in the United States.* Ann Arbor: The University of Michigan Press.

Gordon Nembhard, J. (2008). Alternative Economics--a Missing Component in the African American Studies Curriculum. *Journal of Black Studies.*

Hamilton, Derrick and Darity, William (2009). Race, Wealth, and Intergenerational Poverty, *The American Prospect.*

Harris, A. L., and Spero, S. D. (1931). *The Black Worker; The Negro and The Labor Movement.* New York: Columbia University Press.

Hudson, Lynn M. (2008). *The Making of "Mammy Pleasant": A Black Entrepreneur in Nineteenth Century* San Francisco. Springfield: University of Illinois Press.

Inikori, J. (2002). *Africans and the Industrial Revolution in England: A Study in International Trade and Economic Development.* Cambridge: Cambridge University Press.

Insight Center for Community Economic Development, Lifting as We Climb: Women of Color, Wealth and America's Future, Spring, 2010.

Jenkins, Carol and Hines, Elizabeth G. (2005). *A.G. Gaston and the Making of a Black American Millionaire.* New York: One World/Ballentine Books.

BIBLIOGRAPHY

Johnson, H. B. (1998). *Black Wall Street: From Riot to Renaissance In Tulsa's Historic Greenwood District.* New York: Marion Koogler Mcnay Art Museum.

Katznelson, Ira (2006). *When Affirmative Action Was White: An Untold History of Racial Inequality in Twentieth Century America.* New York: W. W. Norton and Company.

Kelley, Robin D.G. (1996). *Race Rebels: Culture, Politics and the Black Working Class.* New York: Free Press.

Ladner, J.L. (ed.) (1973). *The Death of White Sociology.* New York: Vintage Books.

Madigan, Tim (2003). *The Burning: Massacre, Destruction and the Tulsa Race Riot of 1921.* New York: St. Martin's Press.

Malveaux, Julianne (1991). Missed Opportunity: Sadie Tanner Mossell Alexander And The Economics Profession. *American Economic Review,* 81 (2), 307-310.

Malveaux, Julianne (2008). Why Is Economic Content Missing From African American Studies? *Journal of Black Studies,* May 2008; vol. 38, 5: pp. 783-794.

Marable, Manning (1999). *How Capitalism Underdeveloped Black America.* Boston: South End Press.

Marlowe, G. W. (2003). *Right Worthy Grand Mission: Maggie Lena Walker And The Quest for Black Economic Empowerment.* Washington, DC: Howard University Press.

Parker, John (1986). *His Promised Land: The Autobiography of John P. Parker, Former Slave and Conductor on the Underground Railroad* (edited by Stuart Seely Sprague), New York: W. W. Norton and Company.

Robinson, Randall (2001). *The Debt: What America Owes to Blacks.* New York: Penguin Books.

Schweninger, Loren (1990). *Black Property Owners in the South, 1790-1915.* Chicago: University of Illinois Press.

Shapiro, T.M. and Oliver, M.L. (1995). *Black Wealth, White Wealth: A New Perspective On Racist Inequality.* New York: Routledge.

Shapiro, T. M. (2004). *The Hidden Cost of Being African American: How Wealth Perpetuates Inequality.* Oxford: Oxford University Press.

Sowell, Thomas (1975). *Race and Economics.* New York: D. McKay Company.

Stewart, Jeffrey C. (1996). *1001 Things Everyone Should Know About African American History.* New York: Gramercy Books.

Stewart, Julia (1996). *The African American Book of Days: Inspirational History and Thoughts for Every Day of the Year.* New York: Carol Publishing Group.

Tauheed, L. F. (2008). Black political economy in the 21st century: Exploring the interface of economics and Black studies – addressing the Challenge of Harold Cruse. *Journal of Black Studies.*

Walker, Juliet E.K. (1995). *Free Frank: A Black Pioneer on the Antebellum Frontier.* Lexington: University Press of Kentucky.

Walker, Juliet E.K. (2009). *The History of Black Business in America: Capitalism, Race, Entrepreneurship.* Chapel Hill: University of North Carolina Press.

Walters, R. W. (1973). Toward a Definition of Black Social Science. In J. A. Ladner (ed.), *The Death of White Sociology* (pp. 190-212). New York: Vintage Books.

Wilhelm, S. (1970). *Who Needs The Negro?* New York: Burdette Press.

Williams, Horace Randall and Beard, Ben (2009). *This Day in Civil Rights History.* Montgomery, AL: New South Books.

Williams, W. E. (1995). A Tragic Vision of Black Problems. *American Quarterly,* 47 (3), 409-415.

NOTES

NOTES

NOTES

Notes